in the SHADOW of the SIERRA

GHOST TOWNS & HISTORICAL SITES OF THE EASTERN SIERRA: NORTHERN REGION

IN THE SHADOW OF THE SIERRA

Published by Nevada Ghost Towns & Beyond

Editing and Publishing Services provided by Stacey Smekofske, Edits by Stacey
Proofreading by Jo Johnston
Map illustrations by Austin Metz
Book design by TeaBerryStudio.com

ISBN: Hardcover: 979-8-9992388-0-1
       Paperback: 979-8-9992388-1-8
       eBook: 979-8-9992388-2-5

*"The gladdest moment in human life, methinks,
is a departure into unknown lands."*

—*Sir Richard Francis Burton*

CONTENTS

ACKNOWLEDGMENTS

Many people deserve thanks for making *In the Shadow of the Sierra* a reality.

In 2020, I decided my midlife goal was to visit and photograph every ghost town in Nevada and the Eastern Sierra. I had no idea where it would take me!

> **In 2020, I decided my midlife goal was to visit and photograph every ghost town in Nevada and the Eastern Sierra. I had no idea where it would take me!**

I started amassing vast amounts of photos and talked with my longest-term friend, Tara Mayberry, a book designer and owner of TeaBerry Creative. A book was in my mind, but it was too large a project to undertake. With Tara's advice and help, I started a blog and social media. Neither of us realized *Nevada Ghost Towns & Beyond* would become my full-time job. Five years later, the book I dreamed of became a reality. There was never any doubt Tara would design it. She is the one to thank for the beautiful design, layout and supporting me through the process.

When my first book was a seed in my mind, amazing local historians, authors and photographers Karen Dustman and Judy Wickwire asked me to breakfast. Even though I had met both, it felt like they had a goal in mind. The reason for the meeting came out at the end of breakfast: they wanted to know when I was writing my first book.

Still debating which book idea to pursue first, I took my good friend Mike on a day exploring the Carson River Route. We ended with lunch in Markleeville in the 1862 Fiske House relocated from the ghost town of Silver Mountain City. I weighed out all the options in excruciating detail. In his usual direct style, Mike told me to shut up and just do it.

I have met many wonderful people over the years of exploring ghost towns. Many trusted me with sites, knowing I would respect them and uncover their buried history. Thank you to Rick, Jared, and others who took me to lesser-known locations.

When I started exploring, I would take our town SUV or BNT, the Big Noisy Truck. It soon became apparent I needed a more capable off-road vehicle. Steve lives not far from me, but we met online when I was debating vehicle options. Deciding a Jeep was the best for me, Steve searched for the right Rubicon. After I got my Jeep, Honey Badger, he walked me through modifications and repaired the damage she received on my explorations. We became good friends and have taken numerous trips around Nevada and the Eastern Sierra. Steve and his amazing wife, Patty, have become like an extended family. A geologist, ghost town enthusiast, emigrant trail, and train lover, Steve reviewed the book for its technical terminology and historical facts.

Years ago, I came across the website Nevada Expeditions. After I started my site, I reached out to the creator, Austin Metz, and told him how much I enjoyed his work. Austin became my primary exploring partner. While we are from different backgrounds, sometimes it feels like we are the same person. Our friendship has grown beyond ghost towns, and he has supported me through life and the book. I half-joke that if we were teenage girls, I would buy us a heart-shaped split "best friend" necklace. He went above and beyond reviewing the book for historical correctness and grammar.

When I built my website, I thought if you built it, they would come. I quickly learned that wasn't the case, so I started social media accounts. I remember how excited I was when I reached 600 followers. Sliding into 20,000, I have the best readers. I genuinely enjoy interacting with them; they have encouraged and pushed me to stretch my explorations and research. Thank you to all my loyal followers.

Along my travels, I expanded my training. Through various groups, I learned off-roading skills, repairs, and recovery techniques.

A special thank you to Clint and Heidi Smith, Jack Daniel, and the other instructors at Thunder Ranch. If I'm not on the trail or researching, Thunder Ranch is my other happy place. Over multiple classes, I learned about self-protection and emergency medical treatment.

Stanley Paher started my journey to Nevada's ghost towns. Explorers consider his book, *Nevada Ghost Towns & Mining Camps,* the bible of ghost towns. I met Stan a few times over the years. He became a mentor, friend, and a great companion on exploring and camping trips. Stan encouraged me to publish this book, telling me this was the first of many. A very special thank you, Stan, for reviewing sections for historical correctness.

Thank you to all of my beta readers. Your feedback significantly improved the book and motivated me to reach the finish line. A special thank you to authors and historians Jeanne Sharp-Howerton and Karen Dustman, who not only edited but also acted as my emotional support authors.

Thank you to my excellent editor, Stacey Smekofske. Tara recommended her, saying she was the best. During our first meeting, I discovered she was from Nevada, lived not far from where I grew up in Idaho, and loved the desert. Stacey made the process as easy as possible by editing and assisting with the publication. She won my heart when I told her I couldn't reach one site due to washouts. We both loved the story, as it involved several locations and we found a way to incorporate it.

I convinced my mom and dad to take me to my first ghost town, Silver City, Idaho. My dad gave me my love for the outdoors and taking the back road. While my mom might not understand my need to be in the middle of nowhere, she is the first one to support and cheer me on. In the summers while growing up, she was always traveling the west coast, with us in tow.

My family has been my biggest supporter. After I decided to start a website, we discussed at dinner how I would approach it as a regular job and see where it went. They have been there every step of the way, encouraging and supporting me. My son is a history lover and finds interesting stories for me to research. My daughter is my mini-me and always makes sure I take care of myself. Hubby ensures I have everything I might need while on my travels. They hold down the fort when I'm gone, put up with the trips and my incessant talk about ghost towns.

Thank you all!

A NOTE TO THE READERS

At fourteen and a half, I got my driver's license and first car. It's an Idaho thing, and it seemed like a grand idea to teenage me. Even at an early age, I knew vehicles were magical, a combination of freedom and exploration.

In 2000, I married a third-generation Nevada ranch boy. He wanted to see more of the Silver State on our first vacation. Instead of the usual tourist guides, I read Stanley Paher's *Nevada Ghost Towns and Mining Camps*. Using it as a guide, I planned a week-long ghost town adventure. As our family grew, vacations were spent exploring the Nevada desert and Eastern Sierra ghost towns.

I raised my family and ran a business, focusing on others. As the family became more independent, my husband told me this was my time to focus on myself. I was at a loss for how to fill my time. One evening, I announced to the family that my mid-life goal was to photograph every ghost town in Nevada and the Eastern Sierra.

I was an anomaly compared to the other women my age. They purchased sports cars, took dance classes, and headed to the wine country. I bought a Rubicon and pointed it toward the desert. I learned off-roading, recovery skills, wilderness first aid, and self-protection. I traded dress clothes and heels for tactical pants and packer boots.

My Jeep, Honey Badger, is a 2013, 10th-anniversary Rubicon. She earned her name because she does not care what our travels throw at her. Despite everything, she keeps going, just like me.

For five years, I explored ghost towns and historic sites, documenting their history and my travels through my website, *Nevada Ghost Towns & Beyond*, NVTami on social media, presentations at museums and historical societies, articles in *Nevada Magazine* and a show on KGFN, Radio Goldfield, the "Voice of the Old West."

> **I hope you enjoy the photos and history and love the Eastern Sierra as much as I do.
> While it is in the shadow of the Sierra, nothing overshadows its history and beauty.**

In the Shadow of the Sierra is a compilation of my travels along the northern region of the Eastern Sierra. The book covers the 150-mile range from Lassen County in the north to Alpine County in the south.

I hope you enjoy the photos and history and love the Eastern Sierra as much as I do. While it is in the shadow of the Sierra, nothing overshadows its history and beauty.

INTRODUCTION

The Sierra Nevada is an imposing barrier. Running parallel with the Pacific coast, the mountains isolate Nevada and Eastern California from the rest of the state.

The Sierra's rain shadow effect creates a dichotomy between the two slopes. The west side has gentle foothills, lush foliage, and an abundance of rivers and streams. The east side is dry, sparsely populated, and desolate. Snow-covered peaks give way to ragged hills and lead to the desert.

> **The Sierra's rain shadow effect creates a dichotomy between the two slopes. The west side has gentle foothills, lush foliage, and an abundance of rivers and streams. The east side is dry, sparsely populated, and desolate.**

Indigenous tribes, including the Washoe, Northern Paiute, and Shoshone, have long inhabited the Eastern Sierra. They often moved seasonally and left few permanent traces aside from petroglyphs.

For early emigrants, reaching the Eastern Sierra was an arduous journey. When approaching from the west, it was a perilous trek across the Sierra. From the east, it was a two-thousand-mile journey on foot, horseback, or wagon. Today, the Eastern Sierra remains rugged and remote, connected to the West by only a handful of passes.

In 1841, sixty-nine pioneers of the Bartleson-Bidwell Party were the first to travel what became the California Trail. Three years later, the Stephens-Townsend-Murphy Party, consisting of ten families, traveled from Iowa to California. They were the first to cross the Sierra near what would become Donner Pass. Early emigrants sought fertile land, economic opportunities, adventure, and religious freedom.

Emigrants traversed the continent, braving challenges such as crossing the jagged Rocky Mountains and the Forty Mile Desert. An estimated ten percent did not survive the journey: for every mile of the trail, there were ten to fifteen graves, many concentrated in the Forty Mile Desert.

The pioneers' last stop before the final push over the steep and arduous range was the Eastern Sierra. Emigrants rested, purchased supplies from traders, and exchanged worn-out cattle and oxen for well-rested livestock. Only a few remained on the east slope in new settlements at Genoa, Dayton, and Truckee Meadows.

Following James Marshall's discovery of gold at Coloma in January 1848, the rush to the promised land was on. Emigrants, miners, and even military battalions hastened to strike it big. Some set sail around Cape Horn at the tip of South America or across the Isthmus of Panama to journey to the port of San Francisco. Most traveled via wagon trains across the California Trail, forged by the early pioneers.

California mines played out within ten years, and the Gold Rush was a bust. Abner Blackburn discovered gold in Dayton, Utah Territory in 1849, but prospectors only sporadically worked the area. That changed in 1859 with the discovery of the famed Comstock Lode. Henry Comstock and James "Old Virginny" Finney are often credited. It was Ethan and Hosea Grosh who discovered silver in 1857, but they both died tragically before developing their claim.

The tide turned, and fortune-seekers headed east from California to the Comstock Lode. The silver rush was on. The Carson River Route was the main path between the gold and silver fields. It linked Hangtown (Placerville) to Genoa and then the Comstock. With congestion around Virginia City, prospectors expanded their search. Likely, not a hilltop or canyon was left unexplored.

The development of settlements followed the same pattern. A miner would locate a promising claim. He would try to keep it a secret, but celebrated at the closest saloon. Alcohol, sometimes in the form of "tarantula juice," loosened lips. The word spread, and miners flocked to the location, eventually setting up dwellings. The fortunate few had tents; many used what materials were available, building shelters of rocks or even holes in the ground covered in branches.

Business owners set up saloons and brothels, often operated out of wagons and tents. Developers arrived, planning towns and selling land they did not own.

Soon, a town sprang to life. Stores, assay offices, boarding houses, and restaurants opened. Schoolhouses and churches brought legitimacy and permanence, and eventually, the fortunate settlements gained a post office.

Ranchers and farmers tamed the land and provided fresh food, a welcome break from canned and dried goods. Enterprising individuals built the infrastructure needed to support mines and towns. Mills, lumber yards, and kilns soon appeared.

States and local entities awarded toll road franchises to individuals or groups who constructed and maintained roads. In return for their investment, travelers compensated the owners with tolls. Stage lines connected one town with another. Station stops along the route were a combination of rest stops, outhouses, and hotels.

In 1868, the Central Pacific Railroad closed the final gap of rail near Truckee. Railways soon connected towns, mines, and mills. Steam locomotives required water, resulting in water stops that sprang to life every seven to ten miles. Settlements developed around the water towers to offer travelers a respite from their journey.

Mines eventually played out. Some towns lasted for decades or years, while others only lasted weeks. Where there was once a purpose to living in the isolated and harsh shadow of the Eastern Sierra, nothing tied people to the area. Most eventually moved on, taking what supplies they could carry and abandoning the rest. Towns, once thriving with life, became ghosts of their former selves.

All too often, the cemetery was one of the few reminders of a town, abandoned and forgotten. Sometimes, it is well-defined and marked with headstones; at other times, it is only a solitary, overgrown grave, marked with a wooden cross or a rock. The mounds and monuments tell the tale of those who lived and died in pursuit of a dream.

The Sierra rain shadow effect challenged settlers and miners with a lack of water, but now the effect protects the remnants they abandoned. Visitors to the Eastern Sierra can find evidence of its history along the range. Everywhere you look, there is history. Ghost towns, homesteads and cabins, graves, mines, and mills... all in the shadow of the Sierra.

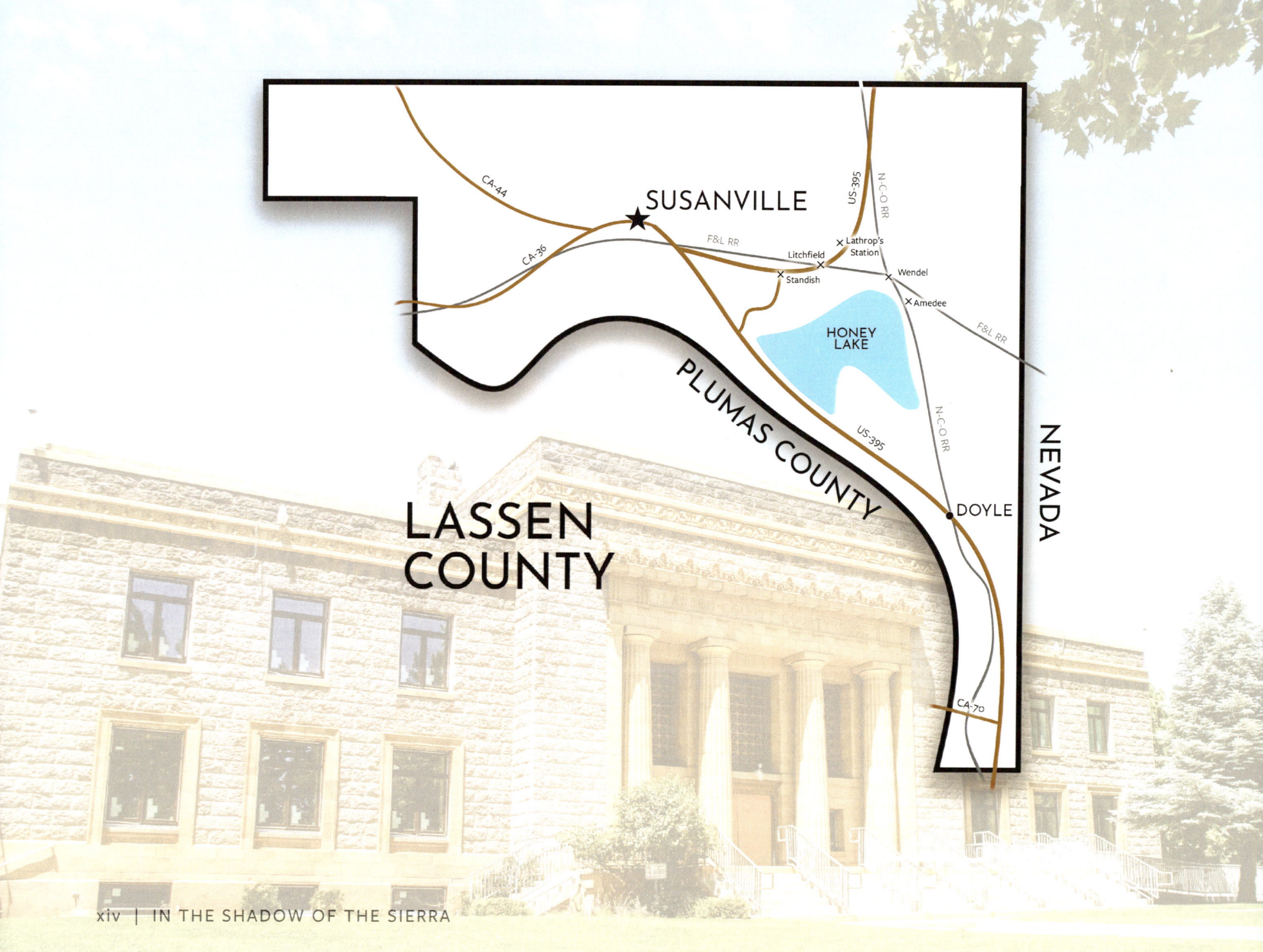

CA-44

SUSANVILLE

CA-36

US-395

N-C-O RR

F&L RR

Litchfield

Lathrop's Station

Standish

Wendel

Amedee

F&L RR

HONEY LAKE

US-395

N-C-O RR

NEVADA

PLUMAS COUNTY

LASSEN COUNTY

DOYLE

CA-70

Chapter One: LASSEN COUNTY

The Gold Rush to the Mother Lode started in the winter of 1849. Emigrants searched for the quickest route to reach the goldfields of California. While many routes crossed the Sierra at Truckee Meadows and Carson Valley, starting in 1846, the Lassen Emigrant Trail ran to the north. In 1852, the Nobles Emigrant Trail became popular as it was shorter and provided access to water and forage.

Isaac Roop established a trading post at the northwest end of Honey Lake, along the Nobles Emigrant Trail. The small settlement of Rooptown grew, later renamed Susanville, in honor of Roop's daughter. Other settlements developed around Honey Lake Valley.

In 1850, the U.S. Congress admitted California into the union as the 31st state. They deemed that the eastern border was the 120th meridian. As there was no survey, many incorrectly assumed the Sierra's crest was the California border and everything on the east side was in the Utah Territory.

Susanville joined the southern settlements of Eagle and Carson Valleys to separate from California and Utah. Isaac Roop and Peter Lassen headed the movement and declared independence, creating the Nataqua Territory. In 1857, a convention in Genoa petitioned to create the Nevada Territory from the Utah Territory, with lands including the Nataqua Territory. Roop was elected the Provisional Governor of Nevada, taking his oath of office on December 13, 1859. Congress created the Nevada Territory in March 1861. Nevada's Lake County included Susanville, which was renamed Roop County the next year.

A survey in 1863 found that much of Roop County was in California. In 1864, the portion of Roop County to the west of the border became Lassen County. The land east of the border, the Nevada Territory portion of Roop County, had only a handful of residents. In 1864, the remaining Nevada portion of Roop County joined Washoe County, Nevada.

Lassen County continued to grow. The Nevada-California-Oregon Railway, (N-C-O), arrived in the late 1880s and transported passengers and freight. Lumber became a leading industry for Lassen County, and Susanville had the largest electrical sawmill at that time. The Fernley & Lassen Railway was instrumental in the county's lumber industry.

FERNLEY & LASSEN RAILWAY

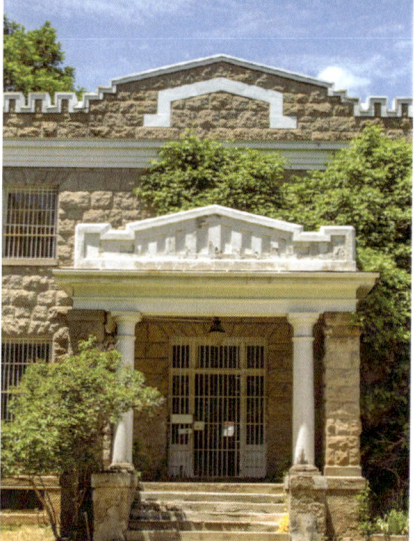

ROOP'S FORT

SUSANVILLE

The uncertainty over the California and Nevada border created confusion in Susanville. Two states with different judges and sets of law enforcement officers tried to regulate the disputed territory and collect taxes.

In February 1863, Plumas County tax collectors arrived in Susanville, but residents refused to pay taxes to California. Plumas County Sheriff E.H. Pierce and his forces crossed the snow-covered Sierra and headed for Susanville. Meanwhile, Isaac Roop and his men fortified themselves at a log cabin known as Roop's Fort or Fort Defiance.

What happened next may be one of the shortest wars ever. On February 15, 1863, each side sent a volley of shots in the direction of the opposition. Only three men were slightly wounded. Witnesses said it was evident that neither side was trying to harm the other.

During the *war*, everyday life in Susanville continued. Spectators arrived to watch the fun. Supporters of both sides gathered at the hotel for a meal, with no hostilities.

Both sides agreed to a truce and ceasefire four hours into the war. The following day, they agreed that two members of each side would present their cases to the governors of California and Nevada. They sent a message to the governors reporting that a "state of war existed between the authorities of Plumas County, California and the authorities and citizens of Roop County, Nevada Territory."

ROOPS FORT
EST. 1854

NOBLES TRAIL - ROOPTOWN
"THIS IS A VILLAGE OF ABOUT 20 HOUSES NEARLY ALL OF WHICH
WERE BUILT THIS SUMMER. [IT] IS SITUATED AT THE HEAD OF
THE VALLEY...THERE IS A HOTEL STORE, BLACKSMITH SHOP AND
...A SAW-MILL NOT FAR AWAY." - ALLEN J. TYRRELL, SEP 8, 1860
GUIDEBOOK AVAILABLE
2006   TRAILS WEST INC. P.O. BOX 12045 RENO NV 89510   N-26

CALIFORNIA TRAIL
NATIONAL HISTORIC TRAIL

JOIN
US AT

PETER LASSEN'S GRAVE

Peter Lassen, for whom Lassen County was named, was born in Denmark in 1800. He emigrated to California in 1840, wanting to farm the rich lands. He established the Lassen Cutoff of the California Trail, which left the main route at Rye Patch, Nevada. Emigrants used the cutoff from 1848 until 1853, when less challenging routes were established.

Lassen was murdered on April 26, 1859, in Black Rock Canyon. He traveled to Hardin City, Nevada, to prospect for silver. Lassen was traveling with Edward Clapper and Americus Wyatt. Lassen and Clapper were shot and killed, but Wyatt escaped, saying a hidden sniper shot them. The attack remains a mystery; theories include that Lassen and Clapper were killed by Paiute Indians, disgruntled travelers on the Lassen Cutoff, or even Wyatt.

Lassen and Clapper's bodies were buried at the site of the attack. In November, Lassen's remains were reburied by a large tree at his ranch outside Susanville. In 1990, rock-hounds discovered a skull and upper body bones, which were later determined to be Clapper's. His remains were reinterred alongside Lassen in 1992.

STANDISH

Standish had a unique beginning. Settlers based the town on philosophy, not mining, ranching, or transportation. In 1897, it became the second settlement of the Associated Colonies of New York. Drawing on the ideals of Plymouth Colony founder, Myles Standish and the economic plans of religious leader Brigham Young, residents were expected to live in town and work in the surrounding fields during the day. Standish recruited Honey Lake Colonial Club citizens to create the Standish Colony.

Legal battles over water rights inhibited the town's growth, but a post office opened in 1899. Standish Hall was built in 1907, with a store on the ground floor and a meeting hall upstairs for various social groups. Neils Mercantile operated into the 1980s, selling groceries, fresh-cut meat, hardware, and work clothing.

STANDISH JAIL CELL

LITCHFIELD

Litchfield was founded in 1914, anticipating the arrival of the Fernley & Lassen Railway. The railroad reached the town in 1913, but it was three years before the station opened. Heard's Market opened in 1948, selling groceries, ranch supplies, and cowboy boots. Litchfield was a shipping hub until 1954, when the depot closed.

LATHROP'S STATION (DAYTON)

George Lathrop and Thomas Harvey opened Lathrop's Station on the Nobles Emigrant Trail. The partners sold the station to the Shaffers in 1862, when it was renamed Shaffer's Station. A townsite was planned in anticipation of the emigrants and the arrival of the Transcontinental Railroad.

A post office opened in 1873 under the name Dayton. When the Transcontinental Railroad never arrived, the town faltered, and the post office closed in 1875.

WENDEL

The Nevada-California-Oregon Railway (N-C-O) built Wendel as a station stop in 1914. Wendel may have changed names more than any other town. In chronological order, the settlement was named Upper Hot Springs, Schaeffer Hot Springs, Smithon, Boyd, Hot Springs Station, Purser, Antola, Caloreta, and finally Wendel.

Just as the town of Wendel had many names, several towns had the name Wendel. Wendel in Lake County, Oregon, was a stop on the N-C-O for a brief time. Both Wendels were named after the friend of Thomas Moran, President of the N-C-O.

Wendel was the junction of the N-C-O and the Fernley & Lassen Railway. The town had an engine house, a water tower, and a powerhouse. The post office closed on December 3, 1993, and the rails were removed except those embedded in the road.

AMEDEE LIME KILN

AMEDEE

Amedee was named after Amedee Depau Moran, a Nevada-California-Oregon Railway (N-C-O) owner. For a decade, Amedee served as a terminus for the N-C-O.

While little marks the town now, Amedee once competed with Susanville and briefly served as the county seat following a disastrous fire in Susanville in 1893. Between the 1890s and early 1900s, it was a main shipping center for ranchers and dairymen because it had the railroad and steamboats to ship goods across Honey Lake. A post office operated from 1890 to 1924.

Amedee was a destination town with hot springs, saloons, gambling, and outdoor recreation, including paddle boats on Honey Lake.

In the early 1890s, the Amedee Lime Works shipped limestone to Reno for processing. In 1893, Charley Falding constructed a stone kiln to process the lime on site. Mining lasted into the 1920s, but despite the high quality of the stone, the remoteness and high shipping costs doomed the Amedee quarry and kiln.

Moving the N-C-O terminus to Wendel led to Amedee's downfall. In 1950, Jack and Margaret Humphrey purchased the entire town for $32.15 ($430 in 2025). They were the only bid at a tax sale.

DOYLE

Doyle was settled in the 1870s and named in honor of Oscar Doyle, who donated land for the town. The Nevada-California-Oregon Railway (N-C-O) reached Doyle on June 6, 1888, connecting the town with routine service to Reno. Around 1898, Henry Butters purchased the Albert E. Ross Ranch in Long Valley and added a church.

William and Rosa Galeppi, Swiss emigrants, relocated from Last Chance (now Frenchman Dam) and purchased the Ross Ranch. The couple had ten children, seven boys and three girls. Rosa renamed the church St. Mary's Chapel Constantia and had visiting Catholic priests hold services. Catholic services were held at St. Mary's Chapel Constantia until 1920.

Doyle's school was housed in the town's church. Grades one through eight were held in a single room, with only three students in a class. In the mid-1940s, a fire destroyed much of Doyle, including the church. Some of the children decided as the school burned, they no longer needed to complete their homework, much to the dismay of the teacher.

The Dixons owned the store in Doyle. They had a hotel on the second floor and a home behind. On hot summer days, children enjoyed trips to the store to play with the owner's twin boy and girl and delight in a special treat of ice cream sandwiches.

In 1994, St. Mary's Chapel Constantia was relocated from the Ross Ranch in Long Valley, five miles south of town, to its current location in Doyle, next to the cemetery.

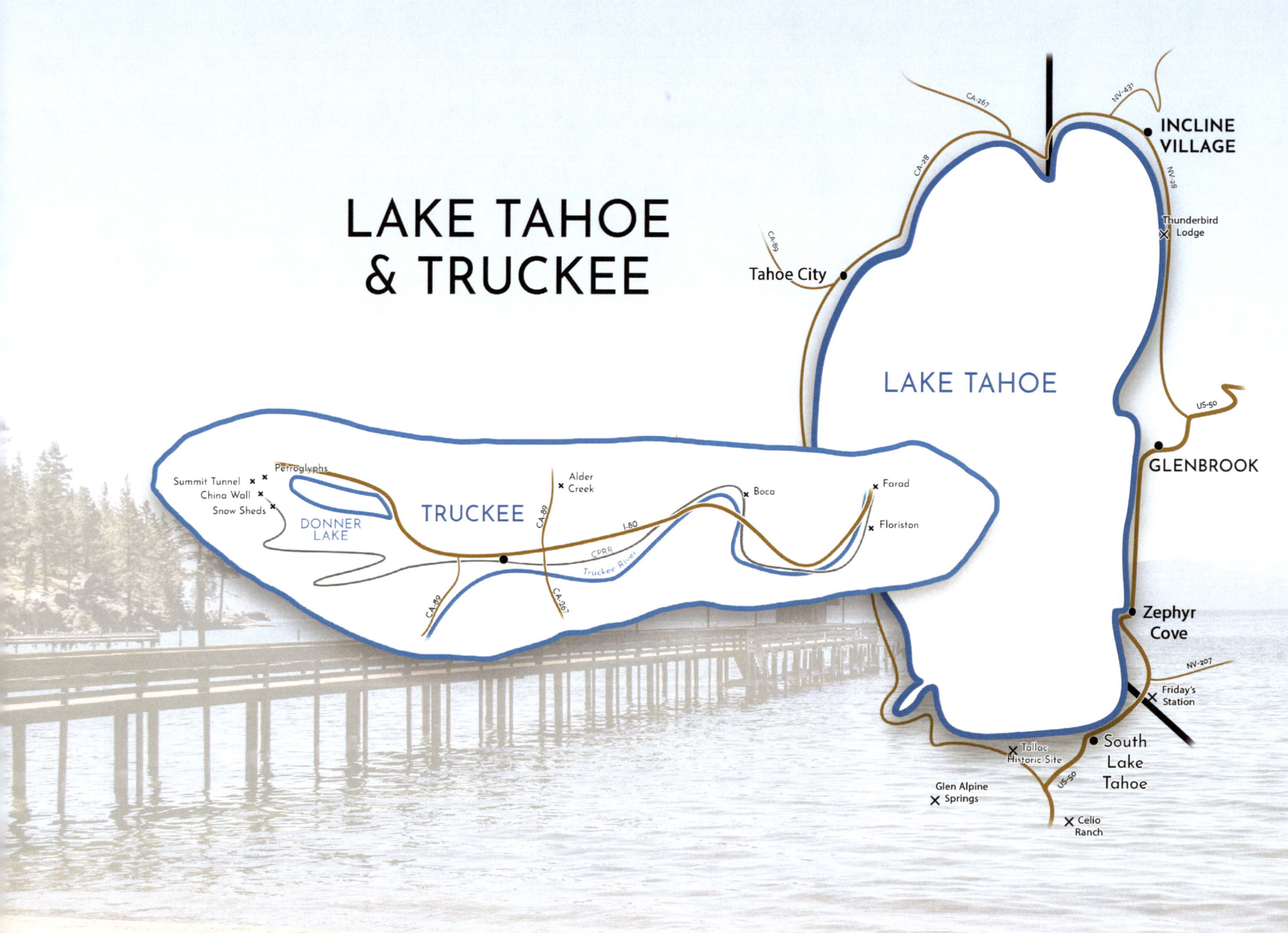

LAKE TAHOE & TRUCKEE

LAKE TAHOE

TRUCKEE

- CA-267
- NV-431
- **INCLINE VILLAGE**
- CA-28
- NV-28
- ✕ Thunderbird Lodge
- CA-89
- Tahoe City •
- US-50
- **GLENBROOK**
- Petroglyphs
- ✕ Summit Tunnel ✕
- ✕ China Wall
- Snow Sheds ✕
- **DONNER LAKE**
- CA-89
- Alder Creek
- ✕ Boca
- ✕ Farad
- I-80
- ✕ Floriston
- CPRR
- Truckee River
- CA-89
- CA-267
- Zephyr Cove •
- NV-207
- ✕ Friday's Station
- ✕ Tallac Historic Site
- • South Lake Tahoe
- US-50
- Glen Alpine ✕ Springs
- ✕ Celio Ranch

Chapter Two: LAKE TAHOE

The Washoe people first inhabited the famous Lake Tahoe, which they called "Da-ow-ga." They camped, fished, and hunted along the lake and basin.

Emigrant routes cut around Lake Bigler, now known as Lake Tahoe. Henness Pass ran to the north of the lake, and the Carson River Route ran to the south. Besides enjoying the scenery while passing through, Lake Tahoe remained mostly undisturbed aside from some early agricultural enterprises.

In 1859, prospectors discovered the Comstock Lode. Underground mining grew so expansive that prior methods of reinforcing walls and ceilings were insufficient. German engineer Phillip Deidesheimer, inspired by a honeycomb, developed a system referred to as square-set timbering. Mines were reinforced with interlocking vertical and horizontal timbers.

Mines needed lumber, and plenty of it, and the main source was the Sierra. V-Flumes connected Lake Tahoe to Carson City to transport lumber. During the twenty-year Comstock rush, the mines used more than 600 million board feet and firewood for mine, and mill engines consumed two million cords.

The Transcontinental Railroad ran north of the lake. Duane L. Bliss owned lumber yards and had a private rail line and steamships.

Lake Tahoe was beautiful despite clear-cutting, drawing people to relax and recreate. Resorts dotted the Lake Tahoe basin beginning in 1861. Most of them have been dismantled or turned into residential or commercial areas.

In the 1880s, the rich and famous discovered Lake Tahoe. Tallac Resort became popular, and families built grand summer estates. Three estates were saved and restored: Baldwin, Pope, and Valhalla. While much of Tahoe was clear-cut, Elias Lucky Baldwin preserved two thousand acres of timber, the only remaining virgin forest.

Lake Tahoe is now a worldwide destination for visitors. While most people come to enjoy the lake, skiing, the mountains, and casinos, history is tucked around the lake in unexpected places.

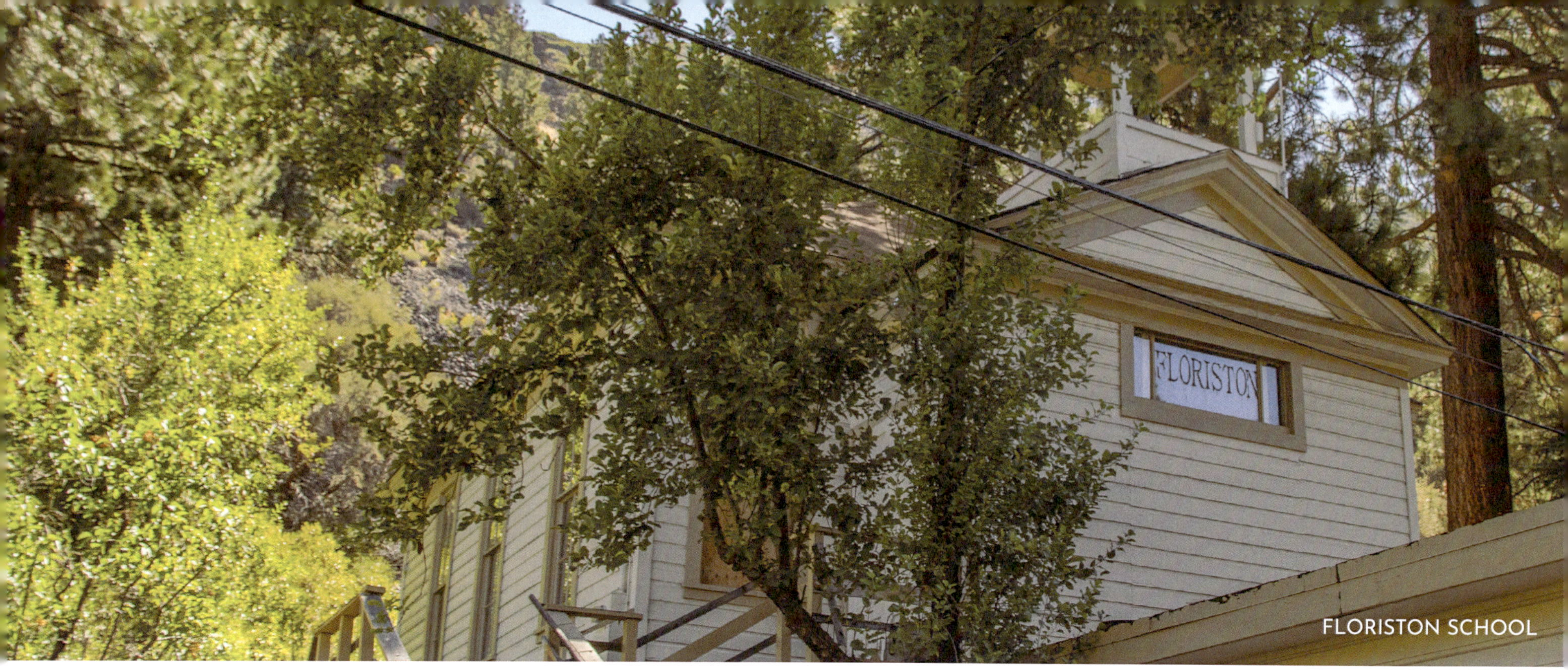

FLORISTON SCHOOL

FLORISTON

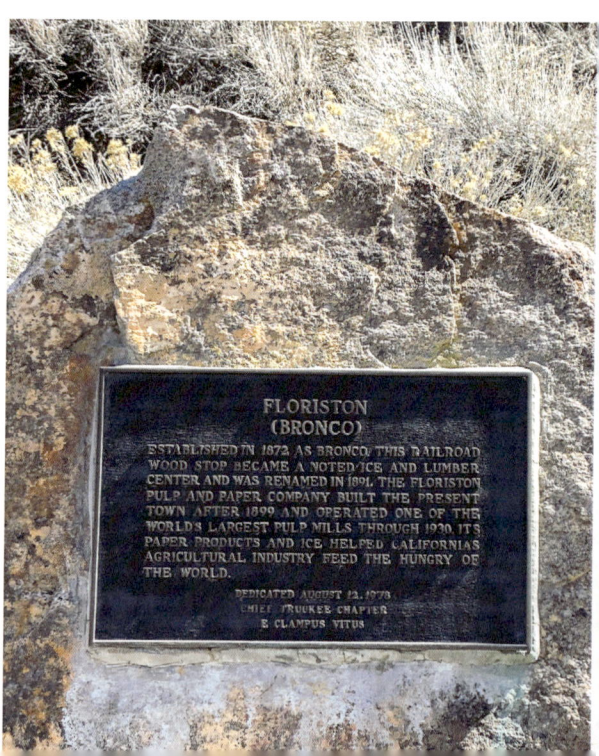

The Transcontinental Railroad operated a construction camp at Bronco Creek in 1867. Between the 1870s and 1880s, the Wicks brothers owned a telegraph office, store, and a lumber yard. Two ice companies operated at Bronco: Rocky Run and Floriston Ice. The town's name changed to Floriston in 1891.

In 1899, the Floriston Pulp and Paper Company built one of the world's largest pulp and paper mills. A company consisted of employee housing, hotel, stores, and a school.

After the mill closed in 1930 due to environmental issues, Floriston became a ghost town. In 1947, Preston Wright, of San Francisco purchased the town. Floriston is now a small community along the Truckee River.

BOCA

Boca started as a construction camp for workers on the Transcontinental Railroad. The Boca Mill and Ice Company began in 1868, and the town became a major producer of ice, lumber, and beer. Fire destroyed the brewery in 1893; the owners did not rebuild. Refrigeration ended the need for ice companies, and trees for the lumber yard soon ran out. Fire again struck in 1904, this time destroying the hotel. Many buildings were relocated; the remaining few were demolished in 1939 during construction of Boca Dam. The post office closed in 1945.

WYNFORD FRANCIS
Son of
Mr. & Mrs. R. C. WEEK
Born March 15, 1906
Died April 2, 1908
Aged 2 Years 17 Days.
OUR LOVED ONE

TRUCKEE POWERHOUSES

Steam boilers initially powered Virginia City's mills. Pinion pines or charcoal made from wood cut locally fueled the boilers. The Truckee River General Electric Company was formed in 1899 and turned its eyes toward the Truckee River. Work began on Farad, the first hydroelectric plant in the Eastern Sierra. The plant produced 1,400 horsepower or 2900 kilowatts, primarily for the mines and mills in Virginia City. Three additional plants followed: Verdi in 1904, Fleish in 1905, and Washoe in 1911. The plants averaged 6.7 megawatts of power to Reno and Virginia City.

The four powerhouses continued operation for more than 100 years. In 1997, a flood destroyed the Farad diversion dam and the plant closed. The remaining three plants continue to provide power to Reno.

FARAD POWERHOUSE

ALDER CREEK
DONNER CAMP SITE

The Donner-Reed emigrant party met with tragedy in the Sierra during the winter of 1846-1847. A heavy storm stranded the party, leaving the ill-prepared travelers snowbound for up to five and a half months. As food supplies depleted, some resorted to cannibalism to survive.

Sixty took shelter near Donner Lake. They wintered in three rough cabins and a lean-to with open doors and rawhide roofs. The Murphy family built their cabin against a large boulder, now located at Donner Memorial State Park.

Due to injury, the Donner family and their teamsters camped at Alder Creek, five miles from the other members of the ill-fated party. The twenty-two at Alder Creek faced even worse living conditions than the rest of the group. They sheltered in tents made with pine trees covered in branches and quilts. As fires sank into the deep snow, they spent days without heat.

The first rescue parties arrived in February; there were four attempts to recover the survivors. Of the eighty-seven members of the Donner-Reed Party, only forty-eight survived.

Some believe the Donners sheltered against this tree. Archaeologists discovered Donner artifacts, including fragments of dishware, the camp hearth, and bones marked by an axe.

DONNER CAMP SITE

TRUCKEE SNOW SHEDS & SUMMIT TUNNEL

In the race to complete the Transcontinental Railroad, the Central Pacific Railroad built a line from Sacramento, California, east 690 miles to Promontory Point, Utah. They had 300 miles fewer to complete than the Union Pacific, which was building westward. However, the Central Pacific had to cross the formidable Sierra Nevada. The railroad grade had to be 2.5% or less, circumvent lakes, and cross the granite range. It was decided to cut tunnels through the mountains. Thousands of men, mainly Chinese, worked day and night in shifts to complete fifteen tunnels. They cut an average of a foot of the new tunnel daily, using hand drilling, black powder, and nitroglycerin.

The Transcontinental Railroad built Summit Tunnel, also known as Tunnel Number Six, between 1867 and 1868. It is 1,659 feet long. The tunnel was completed on August 30, 1867, with the first train rolling through two months later. The highest-elevation tunnel in the world at the time, at 7,056 feet, was a key component of completing the Transcontinental Railroad. Once complete, it began regular passenger service allowing travelers to cross the country in six days instead of the previous 140 required by wagon.

CHINA WALL

The railroads had difficulty finding workers as most men were drawn to the California gold mines and the silver rush in the Comstock. Miners' unions prohibited the Chinese from mining underground, so they worked as laborers, woodcutters, laundrymen, and servants. The railroad recruited Chinese gold miners who had worked in the Gold Country and were later brought directly from China. It was dangerous work, and an estimated 500 to 1,000 Chinese lost their lives.

As railroad workers blasted and dug Summit Tunnel, they moved rubble to ravines along the tunnel. They fitted rocks together to create a 150-foot-tall retaining wall constructed with dry fill.

The rock wall next to the Summit Tunnel is named China Wall. A monument from Truckee Donner Historical Society honors "... these Asian 'Master Builders' who left an indelible mark on the history of California and the West."

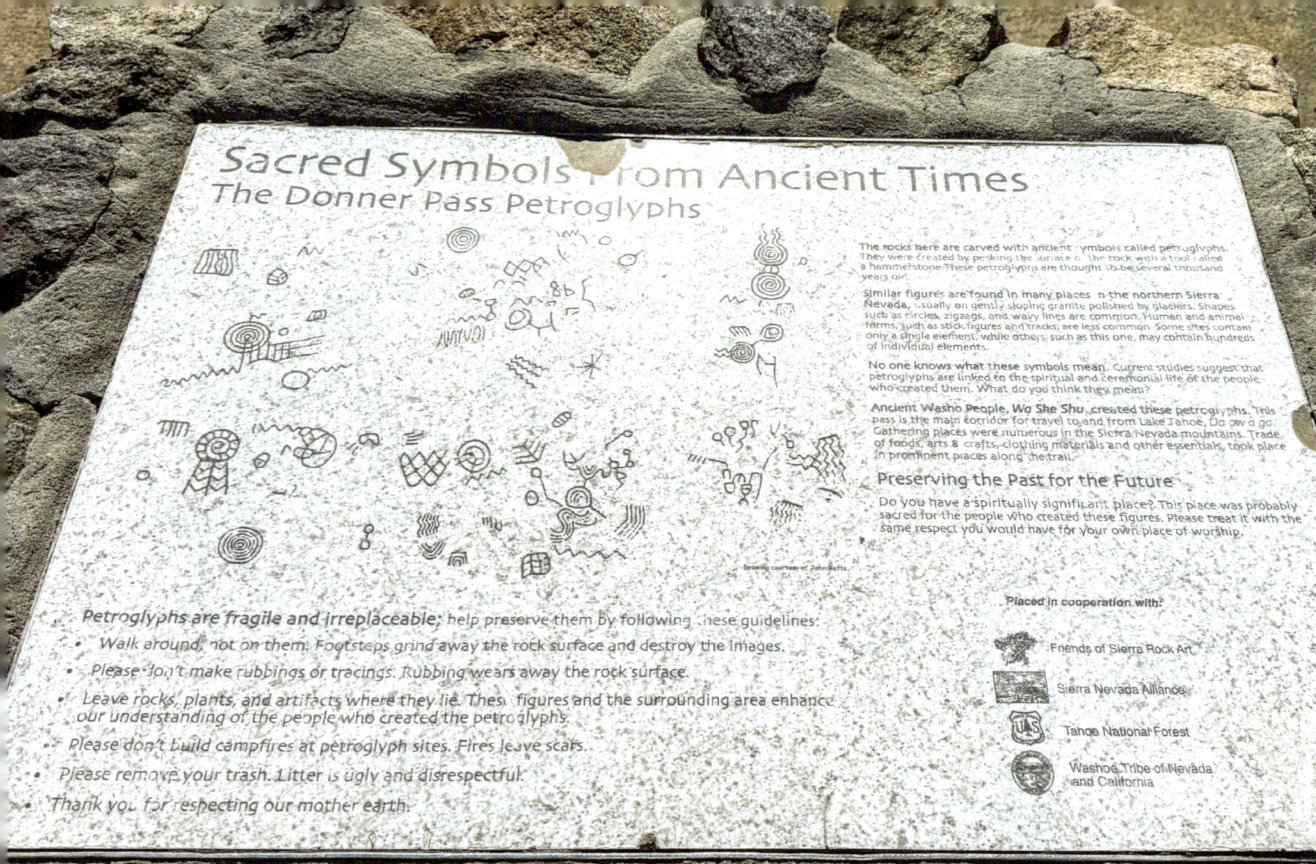

DONNER SUMMIT PETROGLYPHS

Native Americans have left their mark on Lake Tahoe. More than 200 petroglyphs cover the granite rock above the town of Truckee. The petroglyphs were pecked or carved into the surface of granite slabs using a hammerstone. They were made 1,500 to 4,000 years ago by the Martis Culture, possible ancestors of the Washoe.

Most Truckee petroglyphs are geometric, but a few human and animal forms and animal prints are present. Archaeologists believe the shapes have a great meaning to the Martis Culture.

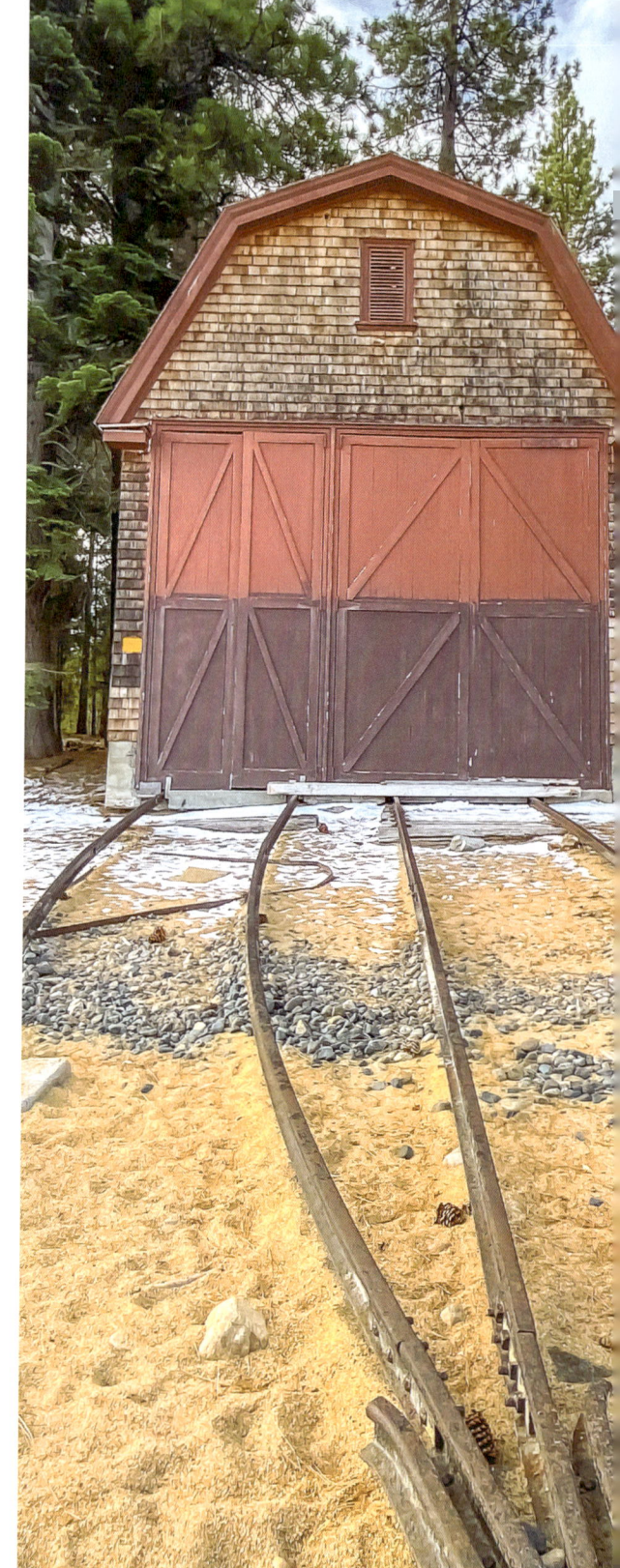

TALLAC HISTORIC SITE

Ephraim "Yank" Clement owned Yank's Station on the Carson River Emigrant Route. He provided services for travelers on the emigrant trail. Once trains crossed the Sierra, wagon traffic declined. Yank purchased eight acres on the shore of Lake Tahoe at Tallac Point. Along with his wife Lydia, they built Tallac Point House. The resort could accommodate forty guests and had a ballroom and campsites.

Self-made millionaire Elias J. "Lucky" Baldwin purchased the adjacent 138 acres in 1872. Yank and Baldwin did not get along, and Baldwin foreclosed on Tallac Point House in 1880. He wanted to serve San Francisco's elite clientele and added to the resort cottages, lawns, beaches, and boats. In 1899, he built a new resort and casino, Tallac Hotel, "the grandest in all the world."

Baldwin leased and then sold private parcels to finance improvements. The resort operated until World War I when it closed. The Tallac Point House burned down, and the Tallac Hotel was torn down in 1920 by Baldwin's daughter, Anita, who wanted to conserve the land. Two original cabins survived, the Anita and Dextra, named after Baldwin's daughter and granddaughter.

George Pope purchased the property in 1923, and his family owned it until 1965. In the 1960s, the US Forest Service purchased private property along Lake Tahoe to increase recreation and access. Tahoe Heritage Foundation repairs and preserves historic structures.

GLEN ALPINE SPRINGS

Glen Alpine Springs opened in 1873 as a health resort known for its soda spring. It soon became a popular place for recreation. Guests enjoyed nature hikes, bonfires, and fishing in trout-stocked streams. Up to 120 guests at a time stayed in cabins or tents. For $5 a day ($150 in 2025), guests were served three meals a day on tables set with linen tablecloths, silver utensils, and china dishware.

During its peak years in the early 1900s, the resort comprised twenty-five buildings, a two-story, sixteen-room hotel, dining hall, kitchen, icehouse, and post office. Most guests arrived via horse-drawn stage after crossing Lake Tahoe, then known as Lake Bigler, by steamboat.

Glen Alpine Springs closed in 1966. The US Forest Service acquired the resort in the 1970s, and Preserve Glen Alpine Springs manages the property.

CELIO RANCH

Carlo Guiseppi Celio emigrated from Switzerland in search of a better life. He arrived at Hangtown (Placerville) in 1853. While he did not make a fortune gold panning, he made enough to purchase dairy cows and land in El Dorado County. During the summers, Celio drove wagons between Hangtown and Nevada via the southern tip of Lake Tahoe, which reminded him of his home in Switzerland.

In 1863, Celio leased a ranch at Upper Lake Valley from Martin Smith, owner of Smith's Station (later Yank's Station, then Meyers). The Celio family drove cattle twice a year between their home ranch and Lake Tahoe for summer grazing.

The Celio family became the cornerstone of South Lake Tahoe. They expanded into dairy, cattle ranching, lumber, blacksmith shops, stores, service stations, and postmasters. Purchasing Meyers in 1903, they applied to rename the town Celio Station, but the post office declined the change.

Over the years, the Celio Ranch added a milk house, slaughterhouse, scale house, horse barn, and wagon shed. A new ranch house in 1914 provided the family with more space.

Through good and bad times, the Celios remained at Lake Tahoe. During financially difficult times in World War I, they were the largest employer, paying their employees and debts on time while allowing debtors to put their purchases on credit.

The beautiful ranch has remained in their possession. With love and dedication, Carlo's great-granddaughter Shirley Taylor restored the property over two decades. Carlos's great-great-grandson Tom and his wife, Chris, have continued this legacy, preserving the property and the family heritage.

HISTORIC
CELIO RANCH

HISTORICAL LANDMARK NO. 500

PARKING →

FRIDAY'S STATION

Martin "Friday" Burke and James Washington Small built the two-story Greek Revival-inspired station in 1860. Friday's or Small's Station was strategically located on Kingsbury Grade, the main pass connecting the Sierra to the Comstock Lode via Carson Valley.

In 1860, Friday's Station became a station for the Pony Express. Friday's was the home station for famed rider "Pony Bob" Haslam. Pony Bob was the first Pony Express rider to use Kingsbury Grade heading east to Buckland's Station. On May 10, 1860, Pony Bob made the ride that made him famous. He left Friday's Station and headed east to Buckland's Station. The rider at Buckland's was afraid of possible hostilities from the Paiutes, so Pony Bob continued his ride to Smith Creek, another hundred miles. After only nine hours of rest, Pony Bob rode back to Friday's Station, arriving only hours off schedule.

On March 4, 1861, Pony Bob made the fastest ride for the Pony Express. He covered 120 miles in eight hours and twenty minutes, while injured, to deliver President Abraham Lincoln's inaugural address.

In 1863, Friday's became a station on the Lake Bigler Toll Road. Between the 1870s and 1880s, the station was known as the Buttermilk Bonanza Ranch. The resort offered "the finest hunting, fishing, and general well-being to be found in the Tahoe Region."

GLENBROOK

In 1860, Captain Augustus W. Pray was the first white settler in Lake Tahoe. He built a log cabin, harvested hay, and planted crops. In 1861, he built a sawmill on the shore of the lake. Glenbrook played a critical role in development of the Comstock Lode, providing lumber for mines and mills. Logs around Lake Tahoe were barged or floated to Glenbrook's four sawmills, producing twenty-five million feet of sawed wood yearly.

The town of Glenbrook supported the lumber and tourist industry. In the warm summer months, 400 lived at Glenbrook. The town included stores, a bowling alley, and a billiard hall. Glenbrook had two hotels, including the popular Lakeshore Hotel. The fine hotel included a dance hall, boats for fishing, and excursions on Lake Tahoe.

The Carson and Tahoe Lumber and Fluming Company, owned by D.L. Bliss transported lumber from Lake Tahoe to the Comstock. Between 1872 and 1898, the company moved 750 million board feet of lumber. Boats were used to ferry logs across the lake. In 1875, the company built the Lake Tahoe Railway. Two Baldwin engines, the *Glenbrook* and the *Tahoe*, each pulled six cars of lumber.

Logging declined in the 1880s and ended by the turn of the century. In 1896, Bliss launched the SS *Tahoe*, a 169-foot, 200-passenger luxury ship with the interior finished in brass, leather, teakwood, and mahogany. Once inhabited by mill workers and tourists, Glenbrook became a haven for the wealthiest Americans.

Samuel Clemens, known as Mark Twain, was the most famous person to lay claim to lumber around Glenbrook. Instead of working hard, Twain and his partners preferred fishing and relaxing on the beautiful lake. Twain is known for saying Lake Tahoe was "the fairest picture the whole earth affords." The partners also enjoyed camping. On one such trip, Twain left their boat and went ashore with bread, bacon, and coffee. After starting a campfire, he returned to the boat for a frying pan. Twain's companion alerted him to the rapidly growing fire. The men fled and watched the devastation from the safety of the water.

LAKESHORE HOTEL

ELEPHANT ENCLOSURE

THUNDERBIRD LODGE

The name George Whittell is not as well-known as Randolph Hearst, but Whittell was once one of California's wealthiest men. In 1922, he inherited $29 million ($550 million in 2025) from his parent's estate, most made from real estate during the Gold Rush. Investing in the stock market, Whittell increased the amount to $50 million ($1 billion in 2025). Whittell withdrew from the market only weeks before the Black Friday crash, maintaining his fortune while many others lost.

Whittell was the ultimate rich playboy. He enjoyed fast cars, boats, airplanes...and even faster women.

Whittell moved to Reno to establish residency and, more importantly, to avoid California's income and inheritance taxes. He purchased 40,000 acres on the shore of Lake Tahoe. His initial plan was to develop the property into a casino and resort. Over time, Whittell decided to preserve the lake's natural beauty.

Although Whittell could have built a retreat to rival Hearst Castle, he opted for a smaller yet still elaborate cabin. Built on the shoreline, his Thunderbird Lodge included secret doors and passageways, an opium den, and an enclosure for his pygmy elephant Mingo. He had the first air conditioning on Lake Tahoe, and a 600-foot tunnel built by former miners connecting the Lodge to the boathouse. The one thing the Thunderbird Lodge lacked was guest rooms; Whittell enjoyed his privacy and didn't want people staying the night. Even Whitell's wife, Elia, rarely stayed at Thunderbird Lodge, as she enjoyed the city's social life and finer things.

Unpaid student masons from the Stewart Indian School near Carson City constructed the lodge exterior and underground passageways. The students added a surprise for Whittell: a miniature replica of the Lodge by the waterfall.

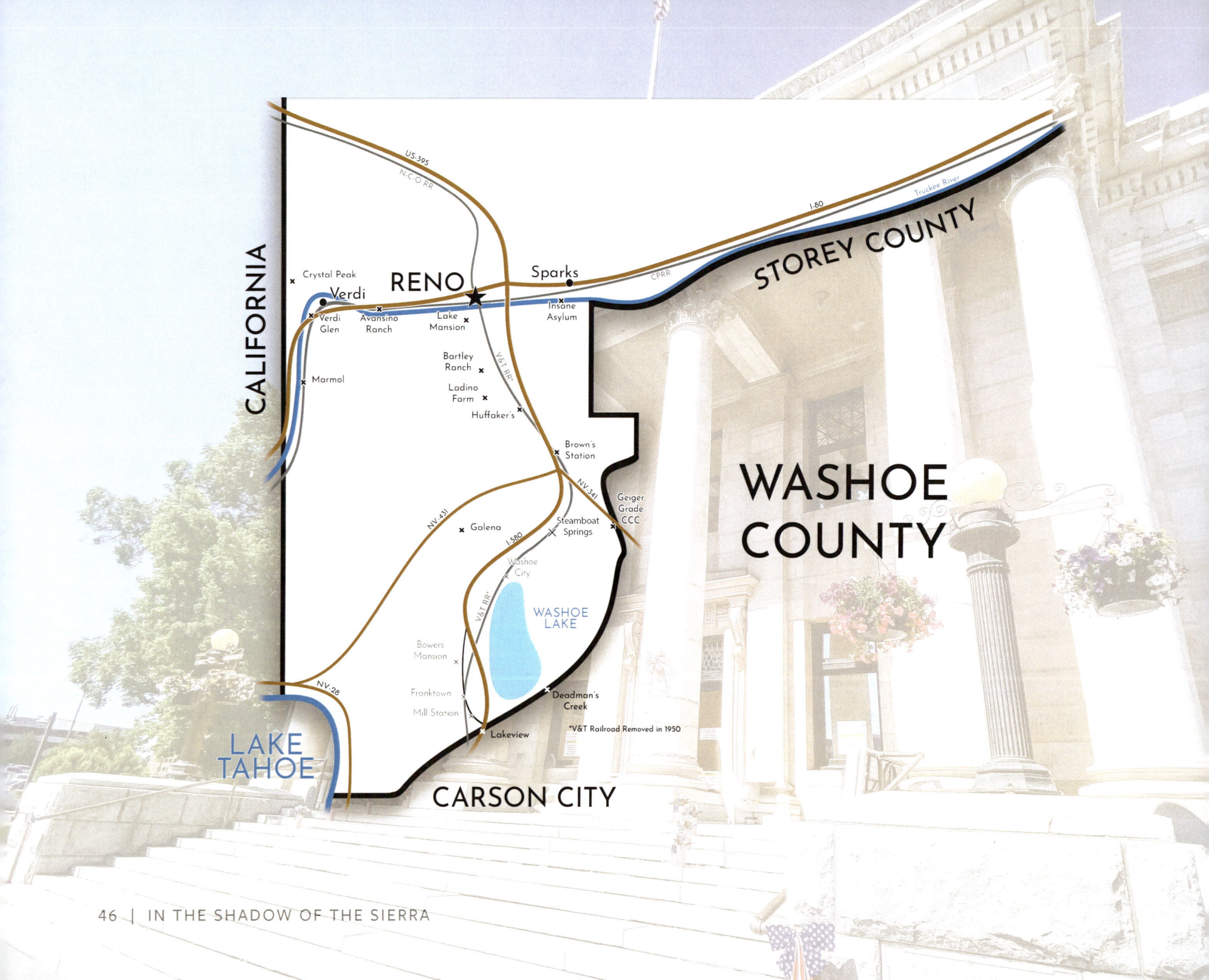

CALIFORNIA

Crystal Peak

Verdi

Verdi Glen

Marmol

Avansino Ranch

RENO

Sparks

Lake Mansion

Insane Asylum

Bartley Ranch

Ladino Farm

Huffaker's

Brown's Station

STOREY COUNTY

US 395

N-C-O RR

CPRR

I-80

Truckee River

V&T RR*

NV 341

Geiger Grade CCC

WASHOE
COUNTY

NV 431

Galena

Steamboat Springs

I-580

Washoe City

V&T RR*

WASHOE LAKE

Bowers Mansion

Franktown

Mill Station

Lakeview

Deadman's Creek

*V&T Railroad Removed in 1950

NV 28

LAKE TAHOE

CARSON CITY

Chapter Three: WASHOE COUNTY

On the journey from the East Coast to the goldfields of California, the Sierra was the last major hurdle to cross. Imagine the relief and dread when emigrants reached Truckee Meadows and laid their eyes on the imposing Sierra. They were so close to California, yet so far.

Jamison (also spelled Jameson), a Mormon trader from Carson Valley, established a trading post in the Truckee Meadows in 1852. Jamison's Station was at a perfect location; due to the river and marshes, every emigrant who traveled the Truckee River Route passed his trading post. Jamison ran a "thriving business trading with the emigrants." He sold food, clothing, tobacco, and other supplies to those joining the Gold Rush.

In addition to selling staples, Jamison traded fresh livestock that could carry the pioneers over the treacherous Sierra. He rested worn-out livestock and fattened them on the rich grass and water of the Truckee Meadows. They were sold to following wagon trains, reportedly at a handsome profit, making Jamison the first to engage in agriculture in the Truckee Meadows.

A handful of pioneers settled on the rich ranch land rather than continue to California. Small settlements formed, including Glendale in 1857 and Lake's Crossing (later named Reno) in 1859.

Truckee Meadows became a major supply center to the silver rush on the Comstock, providing lumber and processing ore at quartz mills. The Transcontinental Railroad arrived in 1868. Lake deeded the land for the new town, which was named Reno in honor of Major General Jesse Lee Reno, a Union officer killed in the Civil War.

Reno became a transportation hub, securing its status as the main center in Northern Nevada. While Reno flourished, smaller settlements were abandoned or absorbed.

AVANSINO RANCH

The Avansino Ranch was deeded in 1869 to the Crystal Peak Hotel and store owner Uriah D. Mastin. In the early 1900s, Lazzaro Avansino purchased the ranch and constructed the stone house. It is now part of the Truckee River Greenbelt and Regional Open Space Program.

CRYSTAL PEAK

The Crystal Peak Company established Crystal Peak in 1864 to prospect gold in the crystal deposits on the nearby peak of the same name. Not finding gold, the town turned to another resource: trees. The company opened the first sawmill in the area. A post office opened in 1864. Crystal Peak grew to 1,500 residents and businesses to support the town and travelers on the Henness Pass Road.

The railroad bypassed Crystal Peak in 1868, signaling the town's demise. In 1869, the post office closed, and service was transferred to Verdi.

VERDI LUMBER COMPANY

VERDI LUMBER COMPANY & VERDI GLEN RESORT

The Verdi Lumber Company harvested and cut trees for use in the Comstock Lode's mines and as ties for the Central Pacific Railroad. Ice was cut from the ponds and stored in ice houses for use during the warm weather. A fire destroyed the sawmill in 1926, and it was not rebuilt.

In 1868, the town of Verdi developed on the rail line. Legend says the name was not for the Spanish word for green, but because a company executive drew the name of the Italian composer Giuseppe Verdi from a hat. Despite two devastating fires, Verdi flourished, drawing business away from Crystal Peak. Beginning in 1924, Verdi Glen Resort was a popular retreat. The facilities included a restaurant, pool, and nightclub. A fire destroyed the resort in 1938, leaving only the pool foundation and an outdoor fireplace.

Guy Marsh purchased the property and built a house on the resort's foundation. In 1993, his wife deeded the property for a park.

ICE POND

MARMOL

The Inyo Marble Works created the town of Marmol in 1890 to house its workers. They named the settlement Marmol after the Spanish word for marble.

The company had a quarry near Keeler, California, but processing the marble on site was too expensive due to a lack of water. Company president, Israel Luce, surveyed along the Truckee River and purchased land from the Southern Pacific Railroad. The location was ideal, with plentiful water and access to the railroad.

Marble processed at Marmol was known as some of the highest quality in the country. It was shipped to California and used in many well-known buildings in San Francisco, including the city hall. The factory opened and closed several times until 1908, when the company dismantled the factory and homes for the lumber.

THE LAKE MANSION

Travelers heading to California through Truckee Meadows needed to cross the Truckee River. In 1859, Mr. Fuller began a ferry service and built a house along the riverbank. In 1860, he built a toll bridge, but it was destroyed by flooding in 1862. Fuller traded the ferry crossing with Myron C. Lake for a ranch in Honey Lake.

Lake built a second bridge in 1863 and added a hotel and saloon named Lake's Crossing. Lake deeded the land to the Central Pacific Railroad, creating a station stop at Lake's Crossing. On May 9, 1868, the Central Pacific Railroad auctioned parcels and renamed the station Reno in honor of Union Major General Jesse Lee Reno, who was killed in the Civil War.

W. J. Marsh built Lake's Mansion in 1877. Lake purchased the beautiful two-story home in 1879. Upon his divorce in 1881, Lake's wife took ownership. The house has been moved twice and is now the Arts for All Nevada office.

BROWN STATION

Peleg Brown, one of the earliest settlers and ranchers in Truckee Meadows, built a two-story house in 1857 in south Truckee Meadows. It had fourteen bedrooms upstairs, which they used as a boarding house. On the main floor, there were sitting rooms, a kitchen, a dining room, and two bedrooms.

On December 20, 1871, fourteen-year-old Henry Jones and his brother, nine-year-old John, stayed the night at Brown Station. The next morning, they continued their journey to American Flats, outside of Gold Hill, herding cattle for their father. Tragically, the boys never arrived at their destination. A search party formed, but storms hampered their efforts. Three days later, on December 24, only four miles from the family ranch, the search party spotted a horse standing near a snowbank. Searchers found the boys' frozen bodies under the snow; the storm had claimed their young lives. Their trusted steed stood over their snowy grave for three days and nights until the search party arrived.

Louis Damonte purchased the house in 1939. In 1995, the house and its surrounding buildings were placed on the National Register of Historic Places, saving them from demolition.

NEVADA STATE INSANE ASYLUM

In the late 1800s, Nevada lacked the facilities to care for those with mental health issues, so they contracted with several hospitals in California to house the Nevada State Insane Asylum. Nevada believed the desert climate would be better for patients. More importantly, they thought care would be more cost-efficient in Nevada than in California. The cost was deemed "cheap enough" at $0.57 a day ($25 in 2025).

Ninety-two acres east of Reno were deeded to establish a state hospital. The facility opened in 1881 as the Nevada State Insane Asylum. The first patients arrived by train from Stockton on July 1, 1882. The 148 patients, 117 men and 31 women, arrived on a special train.

The asylum operated similarly to a poor farm, with the residents raising crops and livestock and operating a dairy. They provided for the hospital's needs and sold excess. They raised hay, vegetables, eggs, milk, potatoes, and even tobacco.

Funding and staffing issues plagued the hospital, causing patients to be lost in the system. The hospital admitted patients for various mental health diagnoses: melancholy (depression), dementia, and chronic mania (bipolar disorder). Other reasons for admittance included losing a business, bad air, lack of food, death of a husband, ardent spirits, "uterine diseases," and the inability to get along with others. Many patients had health conditions related to mining.

The original hospital building was demolished. Later structures remain and are now part of Northern Nevada Adult Mental Health.

Northern Nevada Adult Mental Health Historic
Cemetery, 1882-1949, is the final resting place of more
than 767 people. Although 767 names are
known, their exact location in the cemetery is not.
There are thought to be up to 400 additional interments
whose names have been lost to history.

The individuals buried adjacent to this monument
are the only ones whose remains are identified
with their name.

"THIS IS SACRED GROUND, NOW PROTECTED, IN HONOR OF ALL THOSE
WHO SUFFERED AND PASSED ON, AND IN HOPE FOR THOSE NOW LIVING
WITH MENTAL ILLNESS, TO BE ACCEPTED IN THEIR COMMUNITIES."

NEVADA STATE INSANE ASYLUM CEMETERY

While the Nevada State Insane Asylum discharged some patients, many remained until their death. Employees buried them on the hospital grounds under the cover of darkness while the patients slept in their rooms. There was little ceremony, only crude wood caskets and shallow graves. Markers were simple tin plates. The first recorded death at the hospital occurred on September 7, 1882. William R. Place, aged forty-two, died of Bright's Disease (nephritis). He had been a resident of Esmeralda County, and his brother attended the burial. The last burial occurred in 1949.

As many records were lost, there is no exact number of how many were interred at the cemetery. The hospital buried at least 767 souls in the cemetery, but there are thought to be an additional 400.

In 1949, the Nevada legislature passed a bill to "abolish the use of any cemeteries now located on hospital grounds." While the law prevented new burials, it made no accommodations for the present graves. As a result, it was as if the entire cemetery was erased from history.

In the 1940s, a large ditch was dug through the cemetery. With the knowledge of the state, an excavator dug the 6-foot-wide and 8-foot-deep trench, ripping apart several graves. The remains were then used as backfill for the excavation.

Over the years, multiple construction projects unearthed more bodies and caskets. Graves were relocated multiple times. Grave markers, when present, were lost and switched. Boundaries of the cemetery were lost. Parking lots and a kitchen were built on hallowed ground.

In the 1960s, the cemetery's grounds became Pinion Park Playground. In 1977, while playing, children unearthed human bones. The cemetery is now a dog-friendly park with an exercise area and shelter.

BARTLEY RANCH

In the 1850s, the Dalton Family owned and operated a farm in Truckee Meadows. The Ferretto family purchased the homestead in the 1860s, working it for almost one hundred years.

Boomtown Casino relocated the ranch buildings dating from the 1850s through the 1910s to Verdi for an "Old West" venue in the 1970s. Following the attraction's closure, Boomtown Casino worked with Washoe County Regional Parks and Open Space to preserve the historic buildings. The Reno Rodeo and Western Heritage Center are adjacent to the display.

LADINO DAIRY FARM

The old barn was part of the Ladino Dairy Farm. Max Fleischmann, heir to the Fleischmann Yeast Company, which produces Fleischmann Margarine, purchased the dairy and later donated it to the University of Nevada, Reno, to study purebred stock. Fleischmann also funded the Fleischmann Atmospherium-Planetarium, the first in the world that could simulate various daytime and nighttime atmospheric conditions.

HUFFAKER RANCH HOUSE

HUFFAKER'S

Before Nevada gained statehood, several communities developed in the southern end of the Truckee Meadows. Huffaker's predated Reno and was one of the largest population centers.

The community was named for Granville W. Huffaker, who settled the area in 1858. By the time Nevada became a state in 1864, Huffaker's had 300 residents, a post office, hotels, and later, a stop on the Virginia & Truckee Railroad (V&T).

First used in 1862, the Huffaker Cemetery is the oldest in Truckee Meadows. Developers subdivided the land, destroying many graves. Work was halted to preserve the remaining graves. Many were relocated, but at least twenty-one remain at Huffaker. Family members and residents formed Friends of Huffaker and worked to maintain the cemetery.

GALENA

In 1860, miners discovered silver-lead deposits on the eastern slope of the Sierra in the Steamboat Hills, fourteen miles south of Lake's Crossing (later Reno). Prospectors A.J. and R.S. Hatch organized a mining district and laid out the town the same year. The district was named Galena, "from the abundance of galena ores within its limits." A quartz mill and smelter, one of the earliest in the Eastern Sierra, was constructed, but it was not profitable, ironically due to the galena. The mills continued to operate until 1865, processing ore shipped from the Comstock Lode.

As mining at Galena declined, the enterprising businessmen turned their eyes to another abundant resource of the Sierra Nevada: timber. They built sawmills to provide lumber for use in the nearby mines of Virginia City and the Comstock Lode. Galena grew to support the lumber mills and soon contained five shops, two lodging houses, saloons, restaurants, a justice court, and a school that doubled as a community hall. Galena was known as the "gayest in Nevada" territory, with the lumber workers imbibing at Galena's dozen thirst parlors. Not just any liquor was up to the standards of Galena's patrons; it was fortified with "powerful ingredients" to satisfy the customers.

The winter of 1864 to 1865 was especially heavy. Freight wagons from the Comstock Lode could not reach Galena. Mills developed along the Carson River, east of Carson City, resulting in Galena's mills closing. Fire destroyed a portion of the town in 1865. In 1867, fire combined with zephyr winds destroyed the remaining structures. With the forest depleted from clear-cutting, the town was never rebuilt.

STEAMBOAT SPRINGS

Geothermal activity created hot springs, steam vents, and fumaroles on the eastern slope of the Sierra. Native Americans considered the location a sacred place. As emigrants headed west during the 1849 Gold Rush, they found the springs a welcome place to rest.

In 1859, a structure was constructed with bathing and steam rooms. Felix Monet, a French immigrant, expanded the facilities in 1860. Soon after, a British physician, Dr. James Ellis, constructed a hospital, cottages, and a drugstore. A fire destroyed many of the original buildings in 1867. Steamboat Springs was rebuilt in 1870 and was popular with miners, tourists, and those seeking medical cures.

In 1891, the Virginia & Truckee Railroad (V&T) connected Steamboat Springs to Reno. For a time, Steamboat Springs was the terminus for the V&T and became a transfer point for passengers and freight headed to Virginia City and the Comstock Lode.

In 1925, Dr. Edna Jackson Carver purchased the land and drilled a well for her new hospital. In 1937, she built the Pioneer State Health Hotel. Steamboat Springs became a training and rehabilitation center for men injured while boxing and racing horses.

GEIGER GRADE CCC CAMPGROUND

The Civilian Conservation Corps (CCC) was a voluntary work relief program from 1933 to 1942 to address unemployment during the Great Depression. The program focused on manual labor jobs related to the conservation and development of state and federal lands. It was open to unemployed and unmarried men ages eighteen to twenty-eight.

Completed in 1939, ten to fifteen campsites and a restroom, are spread over a few acres on Geiger Grade. Stairs cut into the rock lead to an overlook. Each campsite had a fireplace made with locally quarried stone. The CCC commonly used stonework in a variety of projects.

OLD WASHOE JAIL

WASHOE CITY

Washoe City was founded in 1860 to supply lumber to mines in Virginia City. Washoe Lake provided hydropower, and mills processed ore from the Comstock Lode.

Dozens of mule freight wagons made daily trips between Washoe City and Virginia City. They transported lumber, food, and other supplies to Virginia City and carried ore for processing on the return trip.

In November 1861, Washoe City became the county seat for Washoe County; on July 3, 1862, a post office opened. The town soon had stores, hotels, saloons, restaurants, and livery stables. Professional services included physicians, dentists, and attorneys. Washoe City added schools, hospitals, churches, fraternal clubs, and a brick courthouse in 1862. At its height, Washoe City may have had 6,000 residents, though many were transients who spent only part of their time in town.

With the completion of the Virginia & Truckee Railroad from Virginia City to Carson City in 1869, mines began to process ore in Empire City along the Carson River. Washoe City's decline was rapid. In 1871, after a legal battle which ended up in the Nevada Supreme Court, Washoe City lost its position as county seat to Reno. Washoe City residents petitioned the legislature to secede from Washoe County and join Ormsby County, but their efforts were fruitless. The population continued to decline, and in 1880 only 200 residents remained. The post office was renamed Washoe in 1894, and service continued sporadically until 1920.

WINTERS MANSION

BOWERS MANSION POOL

PARLOR

BOWERS MANSION

Eilley Orm operated a boarding house at Johntown in Gold Canyon. She was one of few women in the area during the discovery of the Comstock Lode and had divorced twice, which was almost unheard of at the time.

In exchange for rent, a tenant gave her a ten-foot claim of the Comstock Lode. Another of Eilley's tenants, Lemuel Sanford "Sandy" Bowers, owned the adjacent ten feet. The two combined their claims and lives, and Eilley married for the third time. Unlike many who sold their mining rights, the couple retained their productive claims, making them among the first millionaires of the Comstock era.

Like many newly-minted millionaires around Virginia City, in 1863, they built an elaborate mansion to display their wealth. The structure was one of the most expensive in the western United States, costing $400,000 ($13 million in 2025).

Returning to Nevada following a European shopping spree to furnish their mansion, the couple learned their mine had played out. Eilley opened the mansion as a resort to support her beloved home and touted the health benefits of the waters found on the grounds. For a time, the estate was alive with vacationers, dances, music, and parties.

Unfortunately, Eilley could not recover from the financial ruin and lost the mansion in 1876. It went through a handful of owners, eventually falling into a state of disrepair.

In 1902, Henry Riter saw a painting of the Bowers Mansion while drinking at a Reno saloon. Fascinated by the structure, he bought it and forty-six acres, sight-unseen, for $1,000 ($37,000 in 2025). A hard-working man, he amassed enough money to restore the mansion and turn it back into a resort and picnic destination. Over the years, he leased the property as a hotel and a health center, among other things. In 1943, he wanted to preserve the history and turn it into a park, so he sold it to the Reno Women's Civic Club for $100,000 ($1.8 million in 2025). Unable to raise the funds, Washoe County Parks paid the remainder. The Bowers Mansion Restoration Committee worked to restore the property, opening it in 1950 for tours.

FRANKTOWN

In 1852, Mormons settled Franktown on the western side of Washoe Valley. Orson Hyde planned the town in 1855. The settlement town grew, but in 1857, Brigham Young called the Mormon members back to Salt Lake City, anticipating an invasion by United States military forces.

Settlers moved in, and by 1860, Franktown was once again thriving. The town's two mills supported the Comstock ores. In 1872, the Virginia & Truckee Railroad arrived at Franktown. The station was a mixed blessing. It connected Franktown to Carson City and Reno; however, it allowed Comstock mills to transport ore to the Carson River Mills, resulting in Franktown's decline in the 1880s.

TWADDLE-PEDROLI RANCH

John Twaddle purchased 630 acres near Franktown in 1869 for $5,000 ($118,000 in 2025). Twaddle retained the ranch for sixteen years before selling it to Italian-speaking Swiss brothers, Stefano and Anselmo Pedroli, for $3,000 ($70,000 in 2025).

After buying out his brother, Stefano opened a dairy. He supplied miners in the Virginia City Comstock Lode with fresh milk and cheese.

The rancher's most famous visitor was Eleanor Roosevelt. The former first lady visited the ranch in 1943 with her friend, political activist Gertrude Pratt who had been staying at the ranch to establish the six-week residency required to file for divorce.

MILL STATION

Mill Station was a small settlement at the south end of Washoe Valley. It was near sawmills and two quartz mills.

Construction began on the Virginia & Truckee Railroad (V&T) on February 18, 1869. The line would ultimately extend from Reno to Virginia City, with an extension continuing to Minden. In 1872, Mill Station became a lumber stop for the V&T.

Mill Station never grew like neighboring Washoe City. The V&T discontinued the line in 1950, and Mill Station faded into obscurity.

DEADMAN'S CREEK RANCH & GRAVES

German-Swiss emigrant Mathias Fege started a farm in southeastern Washoe Valley in 1860. It consisted of 141 acres and a "lively spring." In 1864, he sold half of the ranch to Jacob Schroeder. The men planted an orchard and garden. They lived solitary lives working the farm. The duo hauled their produce to miners in Virginia City and the surrounding areas.

On June 6, 1865, visitors found the two men dead in their cabin. The inquiry determined they died the day before. It was assumed to be a double murder, but it was later determined that Fege shot and killed his partner and then turned the gun on himself. As late as 1900, speculation about the deaths continued with the Carson City *Daily Appeal* reporting "some unfortunate met his fate there in the early days at the hands of Indians."

As with many sites of the Old West, the truth of what occurred may never be known.

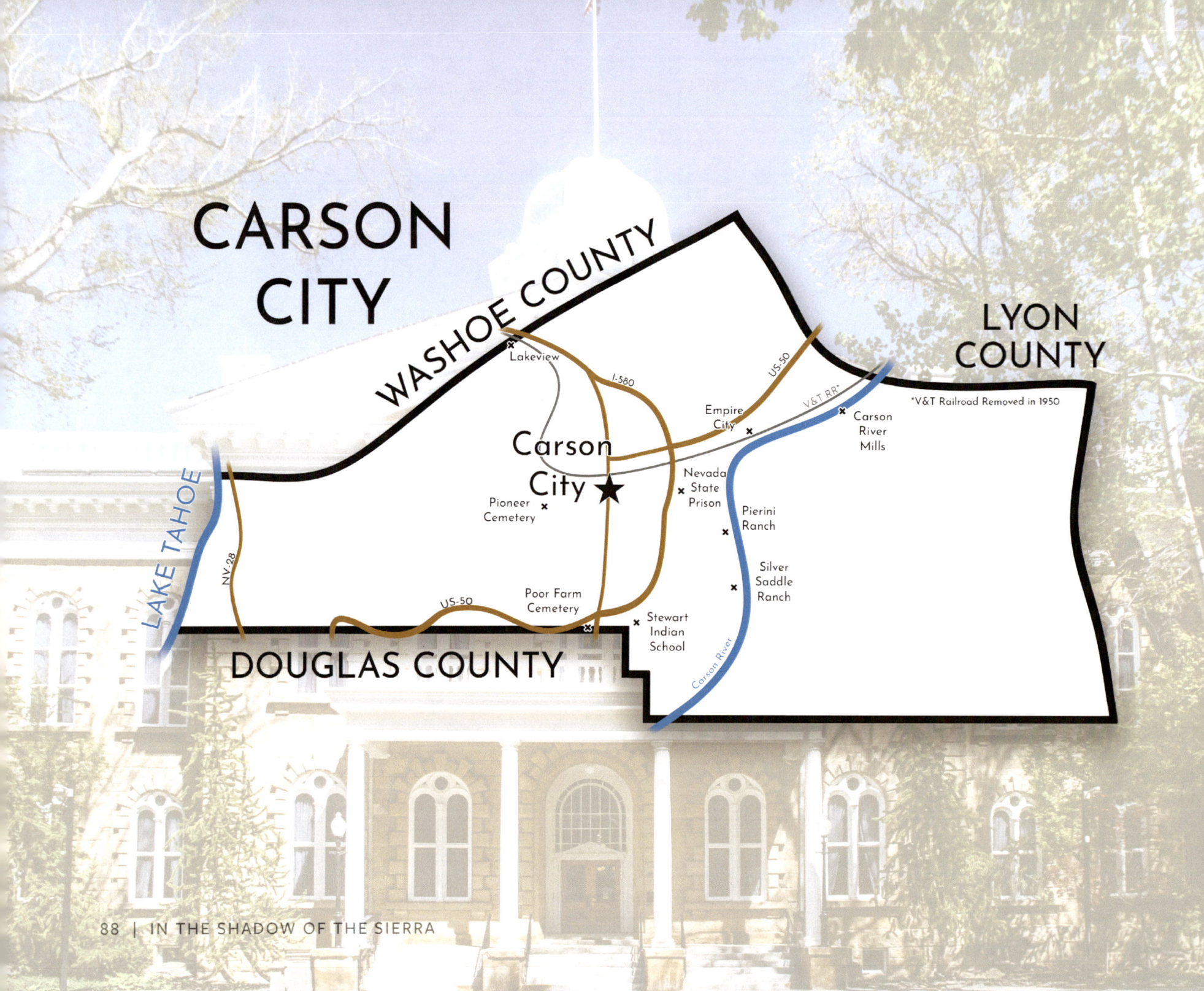

CARSON CITY

WASHOE COUNTY

LYON COUNTY

DOUGLAS COUNTY

LAKE TAHOE

Lakeview

I-580

US-50

V&T RR*

*V&T Railroad Removed in 1950

Empire City

Carson River Mills

Carson City ★

Nevada State Prison

Pierini Ranch

Pioneer Cemetery

NV-28

Silver Saddle Ranch

US-50

Poor Farm Cemetery

Stewart Indian School

Carson River

Chapter Four: CARSON CITY

Between Washoe Valley and Mormon Station (later Genoa), lies Eagle Valley. The valley was abundant with rich ranch land. In 1851, travel increased between the two settlements and partners Hall and Hall, Follensebee, Barnard, and Rollins opened Eagle Station, a trading post to serve travelers.

In 1858, Abraham Curry platted the town of Carson City. Hoping it would become the state capital, Curry set aside ten acres for government buildings. Curry also built the Warm Springs Hotel. When Nevada became a territory in March 1861, Curry's hotel held the first state legislature sessions. In 1862, the hotel became the first possession of Nevada and was used as a prison.

The Nevada territorial legislature created nine counties. Carson City was in Ormsby County, named after William Ormsby, a fatality of the Pyramid Lake War of 1860. Abraham Lincoln granted Nevada statehood in 1864, naming Carson City the capital.

With the silver rush to the Comstock Lode in 1859, Carson City became a thriving commercial center for passenger and freight transportation. The Virginia & Truckee Railroad connected Carson City to Virginia City and the Transcontinental Railroad in Reno.

In 1869, the state legislature authorized the construction of a state capitol. A $100,000 ($2.4 million in 2025) stipend was allotted from a tax levy and sales of public lands. The Nevada State Prison provided low-cost supplies and labor since inmates could quarry sandstone from the prison grounds, which was used to build much of Carson City including the capitol and other state buildings.

The Nevada State Capitol is cruciform with two rectangular wings. A cupola and octagonal dome topped the center. The glass panes are French crystal. Floors and walls are Alaskan marble, cut and polished on site. Prominent Nevada architect, Frederic De Longchamps, designed a northern and southern wing annex for the legislature which was complete for the 1915 session.

In 1966, a statewide referendum approved the consolidation of Ormsby County and Carson City, and a constitutional amendment was passed the following year. On April 1, 1969, Carson City merged with Ormsby County to create the Consolidated Municipality of Carson City. At only 144 square miles, it is the smallest county in Nevada. Until 2017, Carson City was one of only four state capitals not connected by the US interstate system.

THE NEVADA STATE PRISON

The Nevada State Prison was the first building owned by the soon-to-be thirty-sixth state in the Union in 1862. The original prison cells were rooms at the Warm Springs Hotel, owned by Abraham Curry.

Nevada State Prison was built from stone quarried on site by prisoner labor. The high-security prison was designed to house 841 inmates with a staff of 211. When Nevada became a state in 1864, its state constitution named the Lieutenant Governor as the ex officio warden, with the Governor, Secretary of State, and Attorney General comprising the prison board. New legislation changed the power structure, and in 1872, Pressly Hyman was appointed as the new warden. Then-warden Lt. Gov. John F. Denver refused to leave his post or to allow Governor Bradley or members of the prison board access to the prison. Denver said the guards would fire upon anyone who attempted to enter the prison, and if necessary, they would release and arm the prisoners to defend the prison. Denver changed his mind... only after the militia was

activated in March of 1873 with sixty soldiers and artillery.

The Nevada State Prison was the sole designated facility for executions in Nevada. Between 1860 and 1921, hanging was the legal execution method. On February 8, 1924, Nevada became the first state to use the gas chamber when it executed Gee Jon. Unsure if the restraints would hold, they purchased car seat belts to secure Jon.

For those who died at the prison, if their remains were unclaimed, they were interred on the prison grounds. Prisoners cut and engraved headstones from the quarry. The oldest reads, "1876," but many graves are unmarked.

LAKEVIEW

By 1863, James M. Thompson established a small station and hotel at the summit of Lakeview Hill between Washoe and Eagle Valleys. In 1865, it became a way station for Dyer's Toll Road, which ran between Carson City and Steamboat Springs.

Thompson's inn was popular with hunters, fishermen, and picnickers. Sadly, it burned on March 19, 1871, just as Thompson was preparing to lease the building.

The Virginia & Truckee Railroad was completed in 1872, and Lakeview became a flag station, and the town's hotel served as the train station.

In 1873, the Virginia and Gold Hill Water Company built a four-bedroom house on the site of the old inn. In 1878, a small Pelton Wheel under the kitchen sink provided electricity for the house. The wheel remained in place until 1957. The water company maintained a private telephone line so the stations could stay in contact with each other and its office in Virginia City. Captain John Bear Overton, superintendent of the water company, maintained quarters at the house until his retirement in 1906.

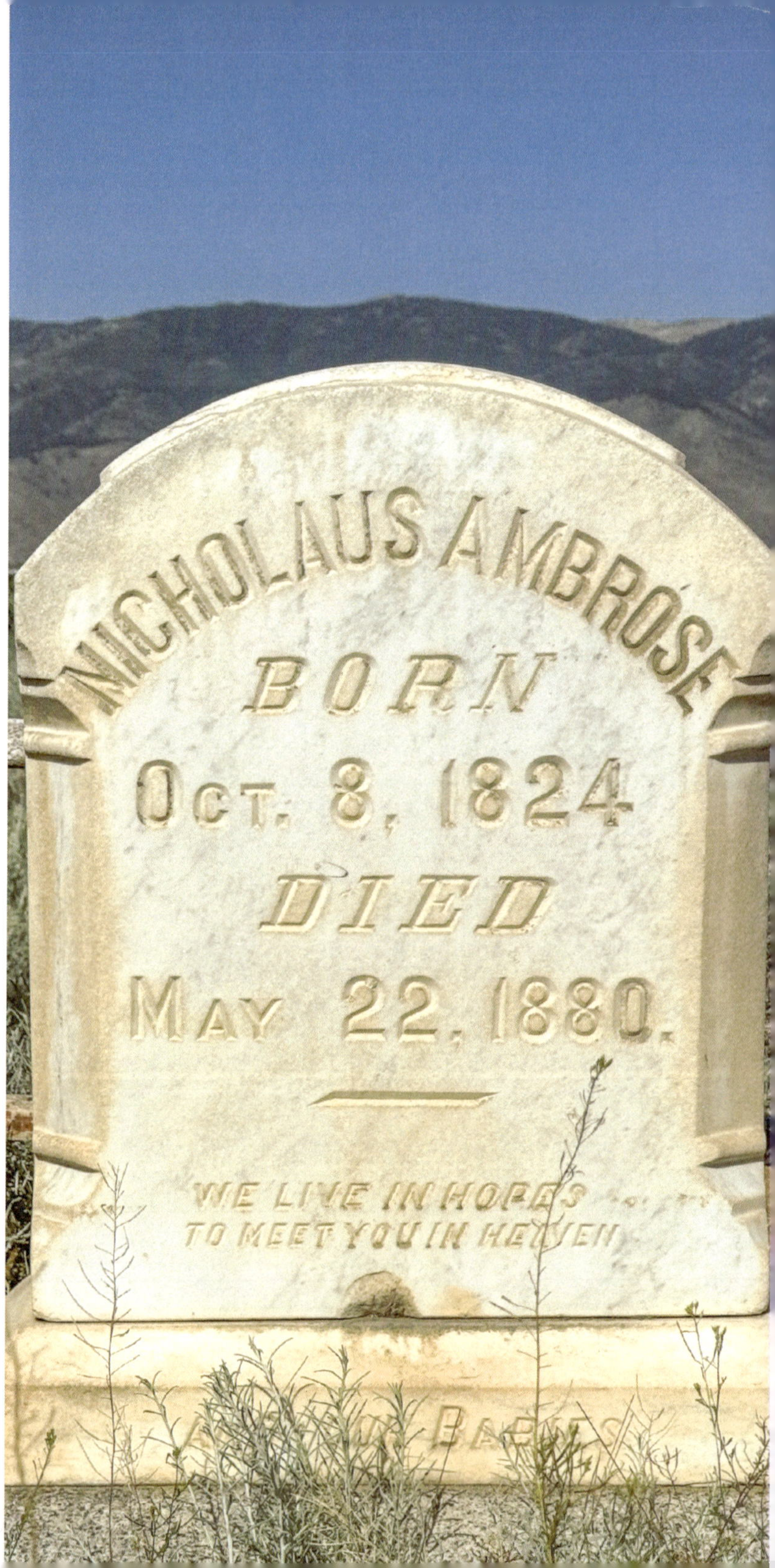

EMPIRE CITY

Once thriving, the only remnant of Empire City is the cemetery atop a hill overlooking Carson City and the superintendent's house for the Mexican Mill. In 1855, Nicholaus Ambrose owned and operated a ranch, station stop, and tavern named Dutch Nick's. The site was on the north bank of the Carson River and a well-traveled emigrant road. Ambrose moved to Gold Canyon in 1857, opening a tent saloon and boarding house. Later, he constructed a small building, which was among the first structures in Gold Hill.

As a townsite, Empire City was surveyed in March 1860. Boundaries of the town stretched more than a mile, including stores, hotels, stables, saloons, a real estate office, and a school. The economy consisted mainly of mining and timber. As Carson City grew, it absorbed the town of Empire.

MERRIMAC MILL

CARSON RIVER MILLS

The Comstock was rich with silver but lacked the water necessary for the milling process. The Carson River was the closest reliable water source, so mines erected mills along the waterway from Carson City to Dayton. The first mill, the Mexican, opened in 1860 at Empire City.

For almost two decades, the canyon was a hub of activity with the mills and housing. Initially, wagons transported ore from the mines to the mills. In 1869, the Virginia & Truckee Railroad (V&T) arrived, dropping ore for the different mills along its route. Estimates vary, but as many as thirty mills operated on the Carson River. The mills along the Carson primarily used stamps to crush ore. Pestles, or stamps, weigh as much as 1,000 pounds each and are usually in groups of five. About twenty to as many as eighty stamps are repeatedly dropped on the ore, breaking it down to a fine powder. Separation of the valuable ore from the powdered rock followed, using mercury, or after approximately 1910, cyanide. The noise was deafening, with stamp mills, trains, and ore crashing down chutes.

Three of the mill sites with ruins are Brunswick, Merrimac, Yerington.

The Brunswick mill opened in 1863-64 and cost $50,000 ($1.3 million in 2025). Initially, it was a ten-stamp mill in 1889 but later expanded to a seventy-six-stamp mill. The Brunswick bridge remains, constructed from two V&T turntables, from Mound House and Steamboat.

The Merrimac Mill was built in 1861 and was one of the largest mills on the river. Destroyed by flood, it was rebuilt farther from the river. It cost $50,000 ($1.3 million in 2025). In 1862, Merrimac employed twenty men.

The third mill started as Blue Canyon, then Copper Canyon, the site is now known as the Yerington Smelter. The V&T laid rail for a balloon track but did not complete the work.

BLUE CANYON MILL

PIONEER CEMETERY

The Pioneer Cemetery is the original graveyard in Carson City. The most notable headstones are Major William Ormsby, the namesake of the county, and Sheriff John Blackburn, the first Nevada law enforcement officer to lose his life in the line of duty.

Major Ormsby was killed on May 12, 1860, in an ambush during the Pyramid Lake War. Ormsby's family exhumed and moved his remains to Oakland in 1880; a gray granite cross marks his original gravesite.

William S. Allen, a scout during the Pyramid Lake War, is buried a few hundred feet away from Ormsby's grave. Allen was killed while leading a scouting party called out by Colonel Haynes. On June 5, 1860, Allen was one of the last fatalities of the War.

On November 18, 1861, Sheriff John L. Blackburn was the first Nevada law enforcement officer to lose his life in the line of duty. He was stabbed to death in the Nicholas Saloon by William Mayfield. Mayfield was found guilty of murder and sentenced to prison, but he escaped. Blackburn was buried along with his friends and Pyramid Lake War veterans, Ormsby and Allen.

In the 1860s, many graves were moved to Lone Mountain Cemetery, but burials in Pioneer Cemetery occurred for another decade. The number of graves remaining has been lost to time.

ORMSBY POOR FARM CEMETERY

The Ormsby County Poor Farm began serving the community in the 1860s. Before federal government programs, including Social Security and Medicaid, counties had poor farms. They were often located in rural areas or on the outskirts of towns. These locally operated farms helped those who were homeless or unable to care for themselves.

J.J. Abraham was the first superintendent of the Ormsby County Poor Farm. In exchange for room and board and a small allowance, residents engaged in chores on the farm. Unlike many poor farms that closed in the 1930s, the Ormsby farm lasted almost one hundred years. Upon its closure in 1965, the remaining residents moved to nursing homes.

Little is left to remind visitors of the property's original purpose. Behind a popular fishing pond, a small, fenced graveyard sits forgotten next to the fairgrounds. Residents' graves were often unmarked or had a simple wooden marker. Two graves have marble headstones as the deceased were veterans of the Civil War. There is no mention of the disposition of the remaining graves. Like many graves in Nevada, they are likely unmarked and lost to history.

PIERINI RANCH

Ranching was a leading industry in Nevada, surpassing mining between 1889 and 1890. At the end of the mining boom, ranching was the lifeblood of railroads. Ranchers raised cattle and sheep.

One such ranch was "The Old Wiggins Ranch," east of Carson City. Dr. John Sullivan owned the ranch in the early 1900s. In 1919, the ranch was leased to two brothers from Lucca, Italy: Salvatore and Pietro Pierini. From 1920 to 1938, Salvatore and his wife Maria resided on the ranch with their three children: Domenica, Angelina, and Pete.

In the 1920s, the family built a stone house to process milk for cream, butter, and cheese. Later, they added a brick oven constructed by two Italian masons. They used the oven for baking and roasting.

The Pierini Ranch Site

In early 1919, two Italian brothers from Lucca, Italy, Salvatore and Pietro Pierini, leased a ranch from Dr. John J. Sullivan. It was called "The Old Wiggens Ranch" and was located east of Carson City, Nevada. Salvatore and his wife Maria operated and lived on this ranch with their three children, Domenico, Angelina and Pete from 1920 to 1938. Angelina and Pete were born on the ranch.

In the early 1920's, an oven was constructed on the ranch. The oven is believed to have been constructed by two Italian stone masons, employed by the Pierini family. The Pierinis used the oven to bake their bread, tortas (pies), various meats and even a whole lamb on Easter.

Next to the oven is a building which was used as a milk house. It was built prior to the oven, however, the exact date is unknown. It contained a machine which the Pierinis used to process the milk into cheese, ricotta (cottage cheese), cream and skim milk for their own consumption.

SILVER SADDLE RANCH

The Silver Saddle Ranch sat on land initially used in the 1860, by the Mexican Mill. The mill was one of the first mills to process ore from Virginia City. Initially, nine employees worked the mill. By 1904, only a handful remained.

Jean Ellissondoberry purchased the land in 1917 and was the first to ranch this area outside Carson City. The ranch was sold several times, with each owner adding additional structures and ranching facilities. In 1997, the Bureau of Land Management obtained the property to preserve open spaces and make it accessible to the public.

STEWART INDIAN SCHOOL

Beginning in 1860, the Bureau of Indian Affairs created more than 400 boarding schools for Native Americans. The federal government forcibly removed children from their families and tribes to assimilate them into European culture. At the schools, they learned English, domestic, and vocational skills.

In 1890, the Carson Indian Training School, the only Indian school in Nevada, enrolled the first student. Soon after opening, it was renamed the Stewart Indian School, in honor of Senator William Stewart of Nevada, who sponsored federal legislation to fund the school.

The school primarily served Washoe, Paiute, and Shoshone tribal children but expanded to over 200 tribes. Up to 400 students attended the school's 240-acre campus. The school was a community, including dorms, cafeteria, auditorium, post office, infirmary, store, and, sadly, a cemetery. The Virginia & Truckee Railroad extended a spur to the school off the line to Minden.

The school was initially a white-frame building. In the 1920s, Hopi stonemasons constructed stone buildings and taught masonry skills to students.

The school's mission changed over the years. Toward the end, students wanted to attend Stewart Indian School, and there was a waiting list. In 1974, a new auditorium opened nicknamed 'Moccasin Square Garden.' The Bureau of Indian Affairs closed the school in 1980.

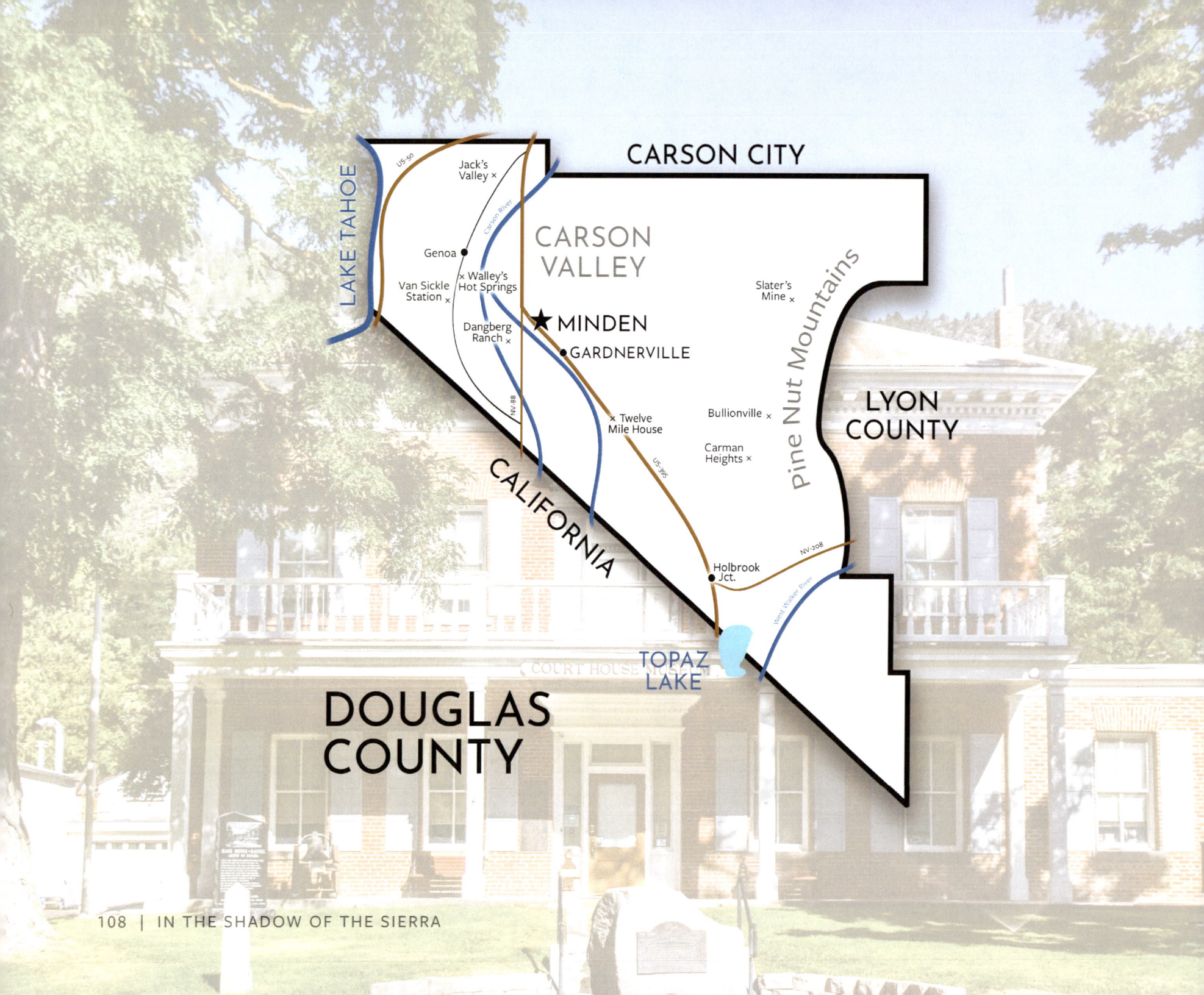

CARSON CITY

LAKE TAHOE

US-50

Jack's
Valley ×

Carson River

CARSON
VALLEY

Genoa ●

× Walley's
Hot Springs

Van Sickle
Station ×

Slater's
Mine ×

★ MINDEN

Dangberg
Ranch ×

● GARDNERVILLE

NV-88

Pine Nut Mountains

LYON
COUNTY

CALIFORNIA

× Twelve
Mile House

Bullionville ×

US-395

Carman
Heights ×

NV-208

Holbrook
Jct. ●

West Walker River

TOPAZ
LAKE

COURT HOUSE MUSEUM

DOUGLAS
COUNTY

Chapter Five: DOUGLAS COUNTY

In 1859, enterprising developers improved the 1847 Carson River Route, developing it into the Amador-Carson Valley Wagon Road. The route connected the Gold Country to the Comstock Lode through the beautiful Carson Valley. The Pony Express used a part of the trail between April 1860 and October 1861. This road remained heavily used for several years until the development of the Henness Route through Verdi.

Douglas County was one of Nevada's nine original counties created in 1861 by the Nevada Territorial Legislature. Carson Valley is the heart of Douglas County, with additional land in Lake Tahoe to the west and the Pine Nut Mountains to the east. To the north is the state capital Carson City (formerly Ormsby County). Ironically, Carson City is not in Carson Valley, but Eagle Valley.

Carson Valley grew as an agricultural center, and towns sprang to life. The fertile ground but short growing season was ideal for ranching and dairy farms. Ranchers provided fresh meat and dairy for travelers on the Carson River Route. In later years, Carson Valley supplied the Comstock Lode and the gold and silver rush around Bodie and Mono Lake.

Toll roads popped up, including the 1860s Boyd Toll Road, which connected Genoa to Cradlebaugh Toll Road, then to Aurora and Bodie.

While ranching was Carson Valley's primary revenue source, miners also prospected the Sierra and Pine Nut Range on the east side of the valley.

The Virginia & Truckee Railroad, "Queen of the Short Lines," arrived in Douglas County in 1906, providing passenger and freight service. The line would continue to serve the communities until 1950.

GENOA

Lying at the eastern base of the Sierra Nevada, the site of Genoa became an important waypoint for the '49ers. By 1850, Mormons built a stockade and corrals and opened a trading post called Mormon Station. The station sold food, clothing, and other supplies to those joining the California Gold Rush. John Reese arrived with twelve wagons, supplies, and stock in 1851 and created Genoa.

Genoa became the first capital of the Nevada Territory in 1861, but it was later moved to Carson City when Nevada became the thirty-sixth state to join the Union on October 31, 1864.

A fire destroyed large portions of Genoa in 1910, however, several buildings survived more or less unscathed, including the courthouse, Masonic Lodge, and the Genoa saloon—"Nevada's Oldest Thirst Parlor." The fort was lost, but in 1947, the Nevada Legislature authorized funds to build a replica. The Nevada Division of State Parks assumed management of Mormon Station in 1957.

JACK'S VALLEY

Following Genoa, Jack's Valley was the next area to develop in late 1851 or early 1852. North of the larger Carson Valley, Jack's Valley was known for its rich ranch land. Multiple ranches were established, including Winters, Jones, and Bell.

Instead of a centralized town, Jack's Valley consisted of ranches scattered around the small bowl-shaped valley. In 1878, the *Daily Appeal* described it as several "calm hamlets."

Today, the valley still contains historical ranches, one of Nevada's oldest cemeteries, and stories of tragic death and murder. In 1872, ten-month-old William "Willie" Fulstone died under "peculiar circumstances." His parents gave him an orange as a toy, and he swallowed a piece of the peel. He didn't choke, but the following day he vomited blood. Sadly, the physician said the case was hopeless and he could not save Willie.

Christopher Johannes Hill, better known as Old Hans, was disabled from working in mines. With his savings, he purchased the Pony Saloon in Jack's Valley. On the morning of August 9, 1880, Old Hans was found shot dead. Harry Fowles was found in Rocklin, California, with Old Hans's watch. He was arrested and transported to jail in Genoa. During his incarceration, he dug a hole through the jail cell and escaped, never to be seen again.

HANGING TREE

In late November 1897, a night of drinking at a saloon in Millerville, north of Gardnerville, turned deadly. Adam Uber of Calaveras, California, had a few too many when popular local teamster Hans Anderson began to torment him for his evening's entertainment. At some point, Anderson grabbed Uber and was shot for his troubles. Anderson met his end, dying on the bathroom floor. Uber was arrested and taken to the Genoa jail. Sobering up the following day, he claimed not to remember anything of the previous night. A week later, on the morning of the 25th at 2:00 a.m., Thanksgiving Day, vigilantes appeared, held the sheriff and undersheriff at gunpoint, and dragged Uber from his cell.

The mob beat Uber and took him half a mile down Genoa Lane to a stand of cottonwood trees. Throwing a noose over a low branch, they hanged him. With his last words, Uber cursed his killers to seven generations.

It seems Uber had his revenge. Soon after the killing, several members of the mob met untimely deaths, one dying in a runaway horse accident at the base of the hanging tree. The town residents cut down the branch where Uber was hanged, but the curse seemed to continue.

WALLEY'S HOT SPRINGS

In the late 1800s, hot springs became popular. Visitors believed the warm waters, minerals, and fresh air offered various health benefits. Some hot springs even advertised healing "secondary sins."

David Walley began his enterprise by using a natural hot spring located a mile and a half south of Genoa and charging fifty cents a bath. In 1862, Walley and his wife, Harriet, built a forty-room luxury hotel with eleven baths and a swimming pool. Walley's establishment became famous among Virginia City's elite and was known for curing rheumatism, tuberculosis, and syphilis. The Walleys sold the property in 1896, but the resort remained popular for over seventy years.

One famous guest at Walley's Hot Springs was Lester Joseph Gillis, better known as "Baby Face Nelson." In 1934, following a sentence to Joliet Penitentiary for felonious bank robbery, during a prison transfer, he assaulted the guard and went on the lam. Nelson's mob connections helped him relocate to the West Coast. Old ways are difficult to change; Nelson used Reno as a base for bank robberies across the country. Following the killing of a federal agent, the FBI named Nelson and his gang as "Public Enemy Number One." With the heat turned up, Nelson fled to the warm waters of Walley's Hot Springs.

Nelson, his wife, and other mob affiliates hid at Walley's for a month, enjoying bathing, dances, and chicken dinners. Tipped off that the law was on to their hiding spot, the Nelson gang fled.

In 1935, a fire destroyed the hotel, leaving only the stone structures: a cool cellar and bath. Walley's owners rebuilt the bathhouse, spa, hotel, and restaurant, which remain popular with visitors.

VAN SICKLE STATION

In 1857, Henry Van Sickle built a two-story hotel, restaurant, store, and bar. Situated on the Carson River Emigrant Route, he provided travelers with supplies and a place to rest before they made the final push over the Sierra.

In 1860, Van Sickle became a Pony Express Station where riders changed horses. Leaving Van Sickle, they followed the trail along the foothills to the next station at Woodfords, California. Kingsbury Grade opened as a toll road in 1860, with Van Sickle collecting the $2 fee per horse and buggy ($50 in 2025). Despite the steepness of the grade, the toll road cut several days of travel off the previous route.

Sam Brown was a local desperado who spent time in San Quentin Penitentiary and reportedly killed eleven men. He supposedly murdered a Faro dealer in Virginia City by cutting out his heart after he dealt Brown a bad hand. In 1861, Brown decided he would

kill Van Sickle to celebrate his thirtieth birthday. Van Sickle didn't take kindly to the idea and dove behind the bar just as shots rang out.

Brown fled south with Van Sickle in hot pursuit. Knowing the terrain, Van Sickle took a shortcut, getting in front of Brown. As Brown arrived at Lute Olds's barn, Van Sickle shot him in the chest, ending his reign of terror.

The court ruled the shooting "Death by a just dispensation of an all-wise providence at his own expense." Van Sickle was required to provide Brown with a burial, including a new suit.

CARMAN HEIGHTS & BULLIONVILLE

Mining in the Pine Nut Mountains expanded in the early 1900s. Ed Carman purchased a two-stamp mill from the Dangberg family. He located the mill two miles below the mines, along Pine Nut Creek. The location was ideal; it was on a hillside to take advantage of gravity, the creek was spring-fed and ran perpetually, and quaking aspens sheltered the small canyon.

One hundred yards above the mill, Carman added a bunkhouse for three miners and a home for himself and his wife, Maud. The mining camp became known as Carman Heights. Other miners lived at the mining camp of Bullionville, below the peak of the mountains near the mines.

By 1913, things were on the upswing. The mill and buildings had been remodeled, and Carman Heights had two bunkhouses. A power plant was purchased from Dangberg and relocated to the Big Frank Mine. A telephone line connected Big Frank and Carman Heights.

By August 1913, a forty-ton mill was operating at Carman Heights. That same year, Carman transitioned from a wagon to a Ford touring car. That first car trip to the mine was difficult; the road wasn't in shape for new-fangled automobiles.

Carman died in 1923, after working the mines for two decades. Pete Brennan assumed control of the operations in 1925, adding a ten-ton mill. On October 21 of that year, Brennan fell 200 feet into a mine and was buried under earth and debris. Recovery of his remains took twenty-one days; the owners decided to close the mine.

SLATER'S MINE

Jerry Raycraft prospected the Pine Nut Mountains on the eastern edge of Carson Valley in 1892 and discovered "good color." On April 18, he filed claims for mineral and water rights at the county seat in Genoa. He named the mine the Buckeye Placer Mine and worked the claim with his brothers. Word of Raycraft's discovery grew, and by August, there were twenty-eight mining claims in the area.

Conflict was inevitable with so many mining claims close to one another. Peter Milich purchased an interest in the Coal Pit claim bordering Raycraft's Black Horse Mine. Milich constructed a small cabin in 1892-1893. The Raycraft brothers destroyed it, claiming it was on their property. Multiple disputes occurred over the next few months, including disagreements over boundary lines and complaints that the Raycrafts were preventing Milich from accessing his water rights.

On May 20, 1893, Milich and an associate approached the Raycraft cabin at the Black Horse Mine. Arthur Raycraft had been ill and ordered the pair multiple times to vacate his property. Milich opened fire with his rifle, and Raycraft returned fire. Neither man was hit, and Raycraft retreated into the cabin and fled out the back of the cabin along with his Chinese cook.

Hearing gunfire, Tom Raycraft returned from moving their sluice boxes. The brothers and their partners fled to Carson Valley, where they notified Sheriff McCormick of the incident. Warrants for assault with intent to kill were issued for Milich and his associates. They were arrested the next day and held in the Douglas County Jail, located in Genoa. Two weeks after hearing evidence, Judge Dake dismissed the case as there were no injuries.

In September of 1911, the mine was bonded by a company organized by concert pianist George W. Slater. Slater and his wife built a stone house and seventeen structures, including a power plant, water supply, and garden. The Slaters were plagued for years with multiple legal issues. Lack of water remained their most significant hurdle.

Unfortunately, the house later collapsed, likely due to severe snowfall. A fire swept through the area, destroying almost everything besides rock and metal.

TWELVE MILE HOUSE

In 1859, Thomas Wheeler built a stage station at the southern end of Carson Valley, where the road begins to climb into the hills. This location was a critical crossroads. The road south continued toward Aurora and Bodie. The road to the west continued to Fairview and Woodfords, where it joined the Carson River Route of the emigrant trail. The road north leads to Genoa, Carson City, and Virginia City.

The station changed owners many times, including with Jack Teasdale. Many mile houses were named after their location on the road or in relation to other stations. Twelve Mile House is twelve miles from the prior stage stop in Genoa and twelve miles from the Cradlebaugh Bridge, where the road crosses the Carson River.

In the early 1870s, Sheriff H.C. Crippen and his wife took over the station. Crippen constructed a two-story hotel; his wife was known for her delectable food. Twelve Mile House became a social center with many dances and parties. Sadly, Crippen committed suicide in 1880.

Fredrick "Fritz" and Margaret Springmeyer assumed the station in 1890. It remained in the family until the U.S. Government purchased it in 1936 when it became part of the Dresslerville Colony of the Washoe Tribe of Nevada and California.

CARSON VALLEY RANCHES

Ranching in Carson Valley started in the 1850s to supply emigrants with fresh produce, meat, and feed for their stock. Ranchers raised cattle, sheep, hay, wheat, and barley. Farmers raised fruit, vegetables, pigs, and eggs. During the silver rush, Carson Valley provided much of the food for the Comstock Lode. A decade later, the valley fed the boom towns of Bodie and Aurora.

Ranches often included the main house, bunk houses for ranch hands, barns, smokehouses, sheds, and shops. If the equipment broke or the ranchers no longer had need, it lay fallow in the boneyard. Buildings were repurposed or abandoned.

The first ranch recorded in Nevada was Ranch One, which John Reese built in 1852. He built a house in the 1850s and a barn in 1874. The house served as a stage stop and the Raycraft Hotel.

In 1909, the Trimmer family purchased the ranch, which remains in the family.

DANGBERG RANCH

In 1853, Heinrich Friedrich Dangberg built a cabin and developed a ranch in Carson Valley. The cabin grew into a house for Dangberg's wife, Margaret Ferris, and their five children. Their ranch grew to include 48,000 acres.

Dangberg's children planned the town of Minden in 1905. They designed the town square around a park and donated land to become the southern terminus for the Virginia & Truckee Railroad, much to the dismay of Gardnerville, a few miles south.

Heinrich's brother-in-law, George Washington Gale Ferris Jr., attended college to become a civil engineer. Returning to Nevada, he worked as a railroad engineer who was interested in bridges. Inspired by a water wheel in Carson Valley, he created the Chicago Wheel for the Chicago World's Fair in 1893, now better known as the Ferris Wheel.

CARSON VALLEY DAIRIES

In 1891, Carson Valley ranchers worked together to create a creamery that allowed them to focus on their herds and ranches instead of processing the milk. That fall, the creamery on William Dangberg's ranch was constructed. It was a large building with a separator room, butter room, and cold storage. Creamery equipment was imported from Germany, and ranchers increased their herds to include milk cows.

Ranchers delivered their milk daily to the creamery, twice a day during the summer. The machines separated the cream from the milk, and the cream was made into butter and cheese and shipped to Virginia City and San Francisco.

The small settlement of Waterloo developed near the creamery. The town included a general store, blacksmith shop, the Creamery Saloon, and a hotel built by C.H. Behrman in 1899. A post office opened in 1907. Waterloo celebrated German festivals, including *Schützenfest* (a target shooting festival) and *Erntedankfest* (a harvest festival).

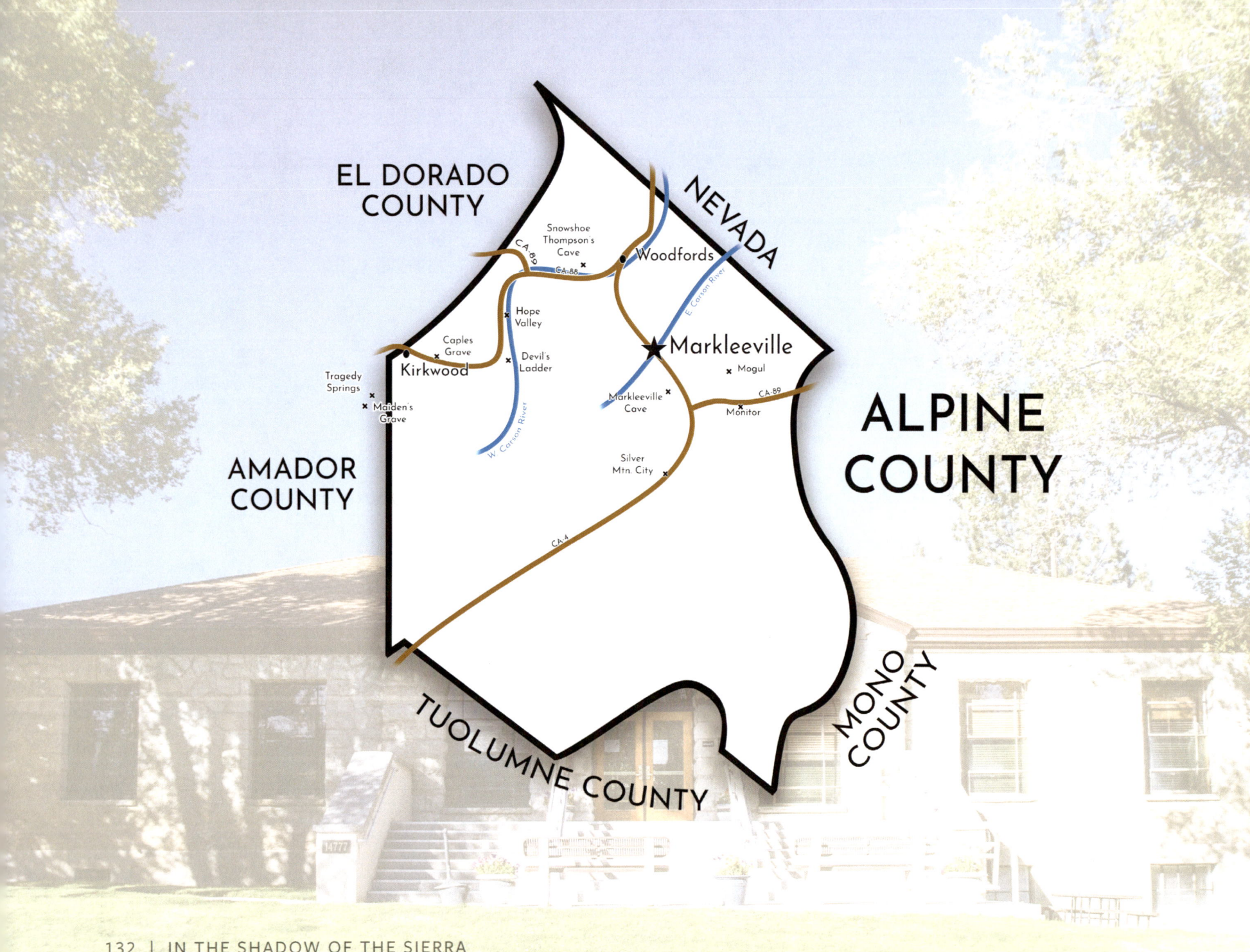

EL DORADO COUNTY

NEVADA

Snowshoe Thompson's Cave

CA-89

CA-88

Woodfords

Hope Valley

E Carson River

Markleeville

Caples Grave

Devil's Ladder

Mogul

Tragedy Springs

Kirkwood

Maiden's Grave

Markleeville Cave

Monitor

CA-89

AMADOR COUNTY

W Carson River

Silver Mtn. City

ALPINE COUNTY

CA-4

MONO COUNTY

TUOLUMNE COUNTY

Chapter Six: ALPINE COUNTY

After the horrors the Donner-Reed Party faced crossing the Sierra Nevada in the winter of 1846 to 1847, explorers were eager to find an alternative to the Truckee River Route. In 1848, the members of the Mormon Battalion, returning from the Mexican-American War, prepared to leave California for Salt Lake City. They learned of an Indian trail about twenty-five miles south of Donner Pass. On July 3, forty-five men, one woman, 150 oxen and 150 horses and mules, seventeen wagons, and two cannons began their journey, hoping to find a better way across the Sierra.

The party gradually moved eastward, encountering steep mountains and rugged terrain. After an arduous journey filled with tragedy, they arrived at the opening of West Carson Canyon on August 4, 1848, and looked out at the beautiful, open Carson Valley.

Word of the new route spread. In the first year, as the trail became known, 500-700 emigrants traveled the new path westward. Quickly, the Carson River Route became the principal trail across the Sierra. Despite the route being higher and steeper than the Truckee River Route, the trail was easier to navigate and required only three river crossings instead of twenty-seven. For the next three years, between 20,000 and 50,000 '49ers traveled over Carson Pass to the Gold Country each year.

With the bust of the Gold Rush and discovery of the Comstock Lode, the tide turned, and more people traveled east over the Carson River Route than ever headed west. As the Comstock became crowded, prospectors spread out, searching for more promising claims. There is likely no canyon left unexplored by miners. Settlements in Alpine County, including Monitor and Mt. Bullion, were thought to be the next great strike. Silver Mountain City became the Alpine County seat in 1864. The mines dried up, and many miners moved to booming Bodie. In 1875, Silver Mountain City lost the Alpine County seat to Markleeville, the main shipping center for farmers and ranchers.

Today, Alpine County is the most sparsely populated county in California, with just over 1,000 residents.

TRAGEDY SPRINGS
(Amador County)

In 1848, the Mormon Battalion, a company of Mormon Soldiers who fought in the Mexican-American War, made their way from Placerville eastward toward the newly established Mormon Salt Lake City, Utah. Many groups were looking for alternatives to the Truckee River Route after the recent horrors the Donner-Reed Party faced.

Forty-five men and one woman began their eastward journey. Daniel Browett, Ezra Hela Allen, and Henderson Cox left the main group on June 22 to scout the trail. Advised against separating but hoping to locate an alternative route over the Sierra, Browett did not heed their warnings.

When Browett and the others did not return, scouts searched, but they returned without success. On July 19, the main company arrived at a spring to find a freshly dug grave littered with arrows. They investigated and found the bodies of their missing scout party. They were riddled with arrows, stripped, burned, mutilated, and robbed.

They dug a new grave and built a rock cairn to protect the bodies. Wilford Hudson engraved a memorial into a nearby tree.

DAUGHTERS OF UTAH PIONEERS

No. 338
ERECTED 1961

TRAGEDY SPRING

THIS CAMPSITE ON THE KIT CARSON EMIGRANT
TRAIL WAS A RESTING PLACE FOR CALIFORNIA
SETTLERS. IT WAS NAMED BY MEMBERS OF THE
MORMON BATTALION ENROUTE TO SALT LAKE VALLEY.
THREE OF THEIR MEN, SERVING AS ADVANCE TRAIL
SCOUTS, WERE MURDERED HERE BY UNKNOWN
PERSONS JUNE 27, 1848. BATTALION FRIENDS,
ARRIVING A FEW DAYS LATER, BURIED THEM IN A
COMMON GRAVE AND CARVED THEIR NAMES
(HENDERSON COX, EZRA ALLEN, DANIEL BROWETT)
ON A NEARBY TREE, THUS PRESERVING THE
GRAVE'S LOCATION.

SACRAMENTO COUNTY

MAIDEN'S GRAVE
(Amador County)

In 1850, young Rachel was traveling with her family to the promised land of California. As was all too frequent, Rachel became ill and perished during the journey. Her family buried her under a fir tree in a meadow.

Fifty-five years later, Rachel's mother returned, attempting to locate her daughter's grave to give her a Christian burial. She was certain she had buried her daughter in the meadow below Tragedy Springs. Campers intrigued by the story assisted in the search but could not locate a grave. Word of the search spread, and in 1908, visitors to Kirkwood Inn located an unmarked grave two miles west of the meadow. Assuming it belonged to Rachel, they started a collection and placed a headstone at the gravesite. A cross with the name Melton previously marked the area, so it was assumed to be Rachel's last name.

Years later, Steven Ferrari was clearing brush from his property below Tragedy Springs when he uncovered a rock outline marking a grave. This spot is considered Rachel's final resting place and is known as "The Real Maiden's Grave."

The discovery of Rachel's grave leaves the question, who is buried at the first Maiden's Grave? It turns out the grave was not that of Rachel-and also not a maiden. It took years of research using emigrant journals, but it appears the original Maiden's Grave contains the remains of Mr. Allen Melton.

DEVIL'S LADDER, ODD FELLOWS ROCK, & THE UNKNOWN PIONEER GRAVE

Carson Pass was the highest point California-bound emigrants traversed on their journey west via the Carson River Route. The steepest slope they encountered was the grade from Red Lake in the east to Carson Pass in the west.

This treacherous section of the trail became known as "Devil's Ladder" and was recorded in nearly every westbound emigrant journal. Devil's Ladder seems impossibly steep, and emigrants used block and tackle to haul their wagons up the slope. Despite the difficulty, in its heyday, more than 250 wagons often awaited their turn to ascend Devil's Ladder.

Emigrants were overjoyed to conquer the notorious Devil's Ladder, many leaving their mark to denote the ascent. In 1849, a group of Odd Fellows left proof of their passage on a group of boulders. One emigrant was not so fortunate. His name and story remain a mystery. He was buried at the top of Devil's Ladder in an unmarked grave. The Independent Order of Odd Fellows erected a monument to "The Unknown Pioneer" in 1950, one hundred years after his death.

HOPE VALLEY

After losing fellow soldiers at Tragedy Springs, the Mormon Battalion arrived in 1848 in a beautiful valley on the east slope of the Sierra. Emigrant journals document the naming, "We called Hope Valley as we began to have hope."

Hope Valley became a resting place for weary travelers. Later, it would become an important crossroads with the Carson River Route running to the east and west, while the Johnson Cutoff split off to the north and the Big Trees Route to the south. The Pony Express rode through Hope Valley for five weeks until Kingsburg Road opened.

James Green settled in Hope Valley, operating a dairy, hotel, and stagecoach stop in the early 1860s. His hotel was an original polling location for Alpine County.

Samuel Alphonse Nott purchased the station around 1869 after Green's suspicious disappearance. Edward Picket assumed the property around 1880, giving his name to Picket's Junction.

CAPLES GRAVE

In 1857, Dr. James Caples opened a physician practice in Hancock County, Illinois. In October 1847, he married Mary Jane Walker. The couple had ten children.

Dr. Caples and his wife gave up the comforts of city living to emigrate to California. On March 21, 1849, they departed with a wagon and three oxen. The couple arrived in Hangtown (Placerville), California, on August 28, 1849. In 1879, he was a member of the State Constitutional Convention in Sacramento and one of the framers of the present California State Constitution.

Dr. Caples passed Twin Lakes on his journey to the Gold Country. He remembered the beautiful lake and purchased property in the area in the early 1850s for a homestead and summer retreat. They raised cattle and started a trading post named Caples Crossing. The station grew to include a hotel and was open only in the summer months.

The family built a blockhouse, using timbers cut and interlocked at the corners, similar to the construction used on Kirkwood Inn. The foundation was approximately twenty by fifteen feet and had a barn. The trading post served patrons for three decades before Dr. Caples moved outside Elk Grove in 1882.

Sadly, one of the couple's children died at Caples Lake. Harry L. was born in 1861 and died in 1864. Harry was buried in a meadow by the lake. In 1922, Caples Dam led to rising lake levels. As the grave would have flooded, it was relocated to higher ground.

KIRKWOOD

Zachary Kirkwood built Kirkwood Inn and Saloon in 1864. It sits on the border of Alpine and El Dorado counties, with the boundary running through the saloon. According to local legend, Kirkwood had a bar on wheels during prohibition. If one county's law enforcement arrived, to avoid arrest, the proprietor rolled the bar into the adjoining county. Being in two counties was also handy in avoiding taxes and the discovery of the slot machine hidden in the kitchen.

After 156 years, Kirkwood is still a popular restaurant and hangout spot. In the summer, they have a variety of events.

WOODFORDS

In 1847, while traveling to Salt Lake City, Sam Brannan left supplies near a spring at the mouth of West Carson Canyon. The location was on the Emigrant Trail's Carson River Route, where the mountainous road opened into the Carson Valley. Brannan Springs grew and became the first European settlement in the area.

In 1854, Willis P. Merrill opened a store in what is now called the Wade House. The Wade House still stands and is the oldest continuously inhabited house in the Eastern Sierra. Merrill operated the store at this location until he built a store on leased land farther west of town.

When a post office opened in 1858, the town changed its name to Cary's Mill. The name was changed again in 1869 to Woodfords due to the proximity to a hotel owned by Daniel Woodford.

On April 4, 1860, Cary's barn in Woodfords became a remount station for the Pony Express. This lasted for a brief five weeks until the Pony Express was rerouted to Kingsbury Grade.

SNOWSHOE THOMPSON'S CAVE

Snowshoe Thompson is known as the "Viking of the Sierra" and the father of skiing in the Sierra. Between 1856 and 1876, John Albert "Snowshoe Thompson" delivered mail across the Sierra from Placerville, California, to Genoa, Nevada. He later added trips to Virginia City, Nevada.

A round-trip took Snowshoe Thompson five days of travel, two days of skiing going west, and three days for the return trip. He consistently made the round-trip two to four times a month, carrying not only mail but also clothing, books, tools, medicine, and supplies like cookware. His pack could weigh up to 100 pounds. He had a series of caves he used as shelter during bad weather. Local legend says this cave was one of his shelters. It is surprisingly large, and soot from past fires still marks the ceiling.

Snowshoe Thompson delivered mail for twenty years without pay. In 1871, he was a delegate to the Republican State Convention in Sacramento, California. A resolution was sent to Washington, DC to reimburse him for his postal service. Despite the resolution and traveling to Washington, DC in 1872, Thompson never received payment for his service.

THE FISKE HOTEL

MARKLEEVILLE

In 1861, Jacob Markley established a toll bridge on the Carson River to connect Silver Mountain City and Genoa. He recorded a claim for 160 acres at Genoa in Douglas County, incorrectly thinking the property was in Nevada.

Markley planned a town and sold lots; the settlement soon included a dozen houses and a boarding house. A post office opened in 1863. A dispute over land ownership in 1863 resulted in a gunfight and Markley's death.

Markleeville became the seat of Alpine County in 1875. The county relocated the iron jail cells from Silver Mountain City, facing them with wood siding. Ten years later, a tragic fire destroyed much of the main street. Business owners rebuilt on a much smaller scale than Markley planned. The Fiske Hotel, which survived a fire that destroyed much of Silver Mountain City three years earlier, was relocated to Markleeville. The little town in the high Sierra fought to survive despite the boom-and-bust cycle of mining and logging.

MARKLEEVILLE CAVE

Silver Mountain City and Markleeville required a road to connect the two mountainous Alpine County towns. Carr and Company, headed by William Johnson, was tasked with building a toll road in 1864.

The new toll road passed near a cave that the Washoe Tribe used as a winter shelter and a ceremonial site. After Tribal Chief "Captain Jim" refused access, Johnson negotiated compensation, which ended up costing $50, a plug of tobacco, and, unintentionally, Johnson's $25 overcoat.

Prohibition lasted between 1920 and 1933. Local lore says those who chose to partake in a nip of hooch and a bit of revelry used Markleeville Cave as a speakeasy.

MONITOR & MOGUL

Silver was discovered in the narrow canyon of Monitor Creek in 1857, but substantial mining and community development did not occur until the early 1860s.

Monitor was named after the Civil War ship USS *Monitor,* the first ironclad warship, launched on January 30, 1862. It sank during a storm on December 31, 1862, off the coast of North Carolina. Sixteen of the forty-nine officers and crew were lost.

By 1864, Monitor boasted fifty buildings, including various stores, a Wells Fargo station, a telegraph line to Genoa, and a newspaper, the *Alpine Monitor*. The town grew to contain boarding houses, restaurants, and six saloons to serve thirsty miners. A post office was opened in 1866, and the town had 2000 residents in the 1860s and 1870s. Nicholas Piequet, in 1868, planted hops in the canyon and opened a brewery. The hops were a

variety from the Alsace region of France and can still be seen more than 150 years later, one of the few traces that remain of the town.

Nearby settlements, such as Mogul, also sprang up as soon as new strikes were made. Once the vein played out, the towns quickly died. Building materials and entire buildings were relocated to the next town, often leaving no trace of where people once called home.

Mining declined in the 1880s, and residents drifted away to more lucrative opportunities. The post office closed in 1888.

SILVER MOUNTAIN CITY

Norwegian miners struck a rich silver ore vein along Silver Creek in 1861. The site was five miles northeast of Ebbetts Pass at an elevation of 6,411 feet. Soon, the town of Kongsberg or Konigsberg developed. By 1862, the population had exploded to over 1,000. The Konigsberg post office opened in 1863 and closed briefly in 1864. In 1865, the post office changed its name to Silver Mountain City.

In 1864, Silver Mountain City became the first seat of the newly formed Alpine County. Three thousand people eventually called the mountainous city home. The business included general stores, bakeries, restaurants, hotels, assay offices, and blacksmith shops.

In 1862, Daniel Davidson constructed one of several mills at Silver Creek, just east of Silver Mountain City. Lewis Chalmers, a native of Scotland, purchased the mill and surrounding land for his employer's investment company in 1870. Chalmers left a wife and seven children at home in Scotland to look after the company's activities. Upon arrival, he ordered the men to stop working in the mine and to build him a beautiful white house, which came to be known as Chalmer's Mansion.

Chalmers eventually married his housekeeper, Antoinette "Nettie" Laughton, in 1880, with whom he had two more children. In 1884, Chalmers returned to his homeland to raise money to save his mine and mill. Chalmers never returned to Silver Mountain City and died in Scotland in 1904.

The mines dried up, and many miners moved to booming Bodie. In 1875, Silver Mountain City lost its position as the Alpine County seat to Markleeville. Some of the buildings were dismantled or moved to Markleeville. In 1882, a fire destroyed a good portion of the former county seat.

Nettie Chalmers died in 1913. She was buried in a small pioneer cemetery close to the mansion. Also buried at the site are Lewis and Nettie's young son, Nettie's son from a previous marriage, and Lewis's oldest son from his first marriage.

CHALMER'S MANSION, SILVER CREEK

REFERENCES

NEWSPAPERS

Indian Valley Record, March 2, 1939

The Daily Appeal Dec 4, 1900: December Hay Making

Mono Herald and Bridgeport Chronicle-Union July 21, 1906 Found Dead at Dogtown

The Daily Appeal, June 1, 1893 War at Buckeye

The Silver State, June 2, 1893 Fight over a mine

The Daily Appeal, June 18, 1893 Stevenson—Raycraft

The Oregonian March 10, 1911 Snowslides Deals Death on Heights

Reno Gazette-Journal

Weekly Nevada State Journal, May 19, 1877

The White Pine News, August 16, 1884

Los Angeles Times, December 11, 1950 Opened in 1860s

Mono Herald and Bridgeport Chronicle-Union Mammoth Lakes, California · Saturday, January 31, 1891 A rich silver strike

Mono Herald and Bridgeport Chronicle-Union Mammoth Lakes, California · Saturday, June 12, 1909 Sweetwater

The Peninsula Times Tribune Palo Alto, California · Monday, March 20, 1939 Jim Townsend Publisher

Yerington Times Yerington, Nevada • Sat, Aug 25, 1917 Silverado Canyon

Silverado Mine Yerington Times, December 29, 1926

Famed mine reactivated Los Angeles Times, December 11, 1950

Burke and Cockerell Gold Hill Daily News October 24, 1871 February 8, 1924

Prospects in Mono San Francisco Chronicle San Francisco, California · Thursday, June 04, 1885

The Ventura Free Press Ventura, California · Saturday, December 16, 1876

Dispute about a mine The San Francisco Examiner San Francisco, California · Tuesday, January 07, 1896

Mono Herald and Bridgeport Chronicle-Union Mammoth Lakes, California · Thursday, June 14, 1979

Mono Herald and Bridgeport Chronicle-Union Mammoth Lakes, California · Thursday, August 19, 1982

Old Mine Regino in Mono County is coming back Oakland Tribune Oakland, California · Tuesday, July 21, 1925

Good Outlook for mining Mono Herald and Bridgeport Chronicle-Union Mammoth Lakes, California · Wednesday, November 24, 1920

Our Camp in 1864 Mono Herald and Bridgeport Chronicle-Union September 16, 1976

Riches in Mono Walker Lake Bulletin Hawthorne, Nevada · Wednesday, November 07, 1883

The Sacramento Mine Yerington Times Yerington, Nevada · Saturday, May 19, 1883

Mono Herald and Bridgeport Chronicle-Union Mammoth Lakes, California · Saturday, October 20, 1883

Inyo Items Walker Lake Bulletin Hawthorne, Nevada · Wednesday, November 07, 1883

White Mountain

Mono Herald and Bridgeport Chronicle-Union Mammoth Lakes, California · Thursday, December 29, 1938

Mono Herald and Bridgeport Chronicle-Union Mammoth Lakes, California · Friday, October 08, 1965

Mono Herald and Bridgeport Chronicle-Union Mammoth Lakes, California · Friday, February 04, 1966 Company at Work Mono Herald and Bridgeport Chronicle-Union Mammoth Lakes, California · Saturday, March 02, 1912

Indian Title to Land Simple one in early years The San Bernardino County Sun San Bernardino, California · Sunday, February 02, 1958

The San Francisco Examiner: Gold But How much? San Francisco, California

Thu, Aug 13, 1891 · Page 1

Los Angeles Times, December 11, 1950

Mason Valley News, March 24, 1961

Mono Herald and Bridgeport Chronicle-Union, January 31, 1891

Mono Herald and Bridgeport Chronicle-Union, June 12, 1909

Yerington Times, August 25, 1917

Mono Herald and Bridgeport Chronicle Union, January 5, 1918

Herald and Bridgeport Chronicle Union January 30, 1941

Reno Gazette-Journal April 12, 1883

Reno Gazette-Journal, July 15, 1938

Reno Gazette-Journal August 13, 1942

The Salt Lake Tribune, June 5, 1936

Western Mining History: Silverado Mine

Yerington Times, November 17, 1926

Yerington Times, December 29, 1926

D.Q.C. (March 28, 1864). "Letter from Mono County". Sacramento Daily Union.

Report of Testimony taken before the Committee on Elections of the Senate, in the contested Election Case of Cavis vs. Quint"; "Report of Assembly Committee on Elections relative to the contested Election Case of Orr vs. Davis."; Items 37 and 39 in Appendix to Journals of Senate and Assembly, Thirteenth Session of the Legislature of the State of California. Sacramento: Benj. P. Avery, State Printer 1862.

Other Interview with Barbra Byington

BOOKS

Basso, Dave. Nevada Historical Marker Guidebook. Nevada Publications, 1986. Page 166.

Browning, Peter. Place Names of the Sierra Nevada. Wilderness Press, 1986.

Cain, Ella M. The Story of Bodie. Fearon Publishers, 1956.

California Bureau of Mines. Mines of Alpine, Inyo and Mono Counties, California. 1917.

Canton, Wanda and Richard. Bodie Railway and Lumber Company: Railroad in the Sky 1881-1917. Friends of Bodie Railway and Lumber Company, Inc. 2011.

Carlson, Helen S. Nevada Place Names: A Geographical Dictionary. University of Nevada Press, 1974.

Carson Valley Historical Society. Snowshoe Thompson. 1991.

Chalfant, Willie Arthur. The Story of Inyo. Hammond Press, 1922.

Dangberg, Grace. Conflict on the Carson. Carson Valley Historical Society, 1975.

DeDecker, Mary. Mines of the Eastern Sierra. La Siesta Press, 1993.

Desmarais, Robert. Cero Gordo: My life in the ghost town. 2023.

Dustman, Karen. Historic Alpine: A Driving Tour of Woodfords, Diamond Valley & Fredericksburg Historic Sites. Clairitage Press, 2019.

Dustman, Karen. Markleeville: A Walking Tour. Clairitage Press, 2014.

Dustman, Karen. Silver Mountain City. Clairitage Press, 2011.

Ellison, Robert W. First Impressions: The trail through Carson Valley 1848-1852. Hot Springs Mountain Press, 2001.

Fey, Marshall. Emigrant Trails: The Long Road to California, A history and Guide to the Emigrant Routes from Central Nevada to Crossing the Sierra. Nevada Publication, 2019.

Gamett, James and Stan Paher. Nevada Post Offices: An Illustrated History. Nevada Publications, 1863. Page 134.

Gudde, Erwin G. California Gold Camps: A geographical dictionary of camps, towns, and localities where gold was found and Mined: Wayside Stations and Trading Centers. University of California Press, 1975.

Hastings, Lansford W. The 1845 Pioneers' Guide for the Westward Traveler: The Emigrants' Guide to Oregon and California. Applewood Books, 1845.

Huegel, Tony. Sierra Nevada Byways: 51 of the Sierra Nevada's Best Backcountry Drives. Wilderness Press, 2008.

Irwin, Catherine. Twice Orphaned: Voices from the Children's Village of Manzanar. California State University Fullerton, 2008.

Journal of the Modoc County Historical Society. Volume 4. 1982.

Lincoln, Francis Church. *Mining Districts and Mineral Resources of Nevada*. Nevada Publications, 1982.

Lingenfelter, Richard E and Karen Rix Gash. *The Newspapers of Nevada: A history and bibliography 1854-1979 T*. University of Nevada Press, 1984.

Makley, Michael J. *Imposing Order without Law: American expansion to the Eastern Sierra 1850-1865*. University of Nevada Press, 2022.

Massey et al. *California Trails: High Sierra Region*. Adler Publishing, 2006.

McGlashan, C.F. *History of the Donner Party*. Press of the City Printing Company, 1939.

McGrath, Roger D. *Gunfighters, Highway Men and Vigilantes: Violence on the Frontier*. University of California Press, 1894.

Mitchell, Roger. *High Sierra SUV Trails, Volume 1, The East Side*. Track and Trail Publications, 2002.

Mitchell, Roger. *Inyo-Mono SUV Trails*. Track and Trail Publications, 2003.

Miluck, Nancy C. *Nevada This is our Land: A survey from Prehistory to Present*. Dragon Enterprises, 1994.

Murbarger, Nell. *Ghosts of the Glory Trail*. Westernlore Press, 1956.

Myrick, David F. *Railroads of Nevada and Eastern California Volumes I, II, III*. University of Nevada Press. 1990, 1991, 2007.

Nation, Nyle. *The Pine Nut Chronicle: The History and Adventures of Mining in Douglas County, Nevada*. Pine Nut Press, 2000.

Newton, Marilyn. *Alkali Angels: Recording Nevada's Historic Graveyards*. Carmel Publishing Company, 2004. Page 174.

Nevada Historical Society Quarterly

Paher, Stanley W. *Death Valley Ghost Towns Volume 1*. Nevada Press. 1973.

Paher, Stanley W. *Death Valley Ghost Towns Volume 2*. Nevada Press. 1981.

Paher, Stanley. *Nevada Ghost Towns and Mining Camps*. Nevada Publications, 1970.

Paher, Stanley. *Nevada Ghost Towns & Desert Atlas*, Nevada Press 2020.

Patera, Alan H. and David A. Wright. *Skidoo: Including Harrisburg and Emigrant Springs*. Western Places, 1999.

Raty, Mary Sauer. *Pioneers of the Ponderosa: How Washoe Vallay rescued the Comstock*. Western Printing and Publishing Company. 1973.

Reiser, Marc. *Cadillac Desert: The American west and its disappearing water*. Viking Penguin, 1986.

Riddle, Jennifer E., Sena M. Loyd, Stacy L. Branham, and Curt Thomas. *Images of America: Nevada State Prison*. Arcadia Publishing, 2012.

Salley, H.E. *History of California Post Offices 1849-1976*. Heartland Printing and Publishing Company. 1977

Shamberger, Hugh. *The story of the water supply for the Comstock*. United States Department of the Interior. 1972.

Silver, Sue. *Aurora Nevada's Silent City on the Hill*. Museum Associates of Mineral County, 2011.

Silver, Sue. *Along the East Walker River: An historical perspective*. 2013.

Silver, Sue. *Volume 1. Mineral County Nevada: Mining Camps, Towns, & Places (1860-1900)*, 2011.

Silver, Sue. *Mineral County Nevada: Volume 2, Mining Camps, Towns, & Places (901 and after)*, 2011.

Silver, Sue. *Volume 3: Mineral County, Nevada: Volume, Early Transportation, Stagecoach, Steamboat and Narrow Gauge Rail*. Museum Associates of Mineral County, 2011.

Silver, Sue. *Volume 4: Progress and People*. Museum Associates of Mineral County, 2011.

Silver, Sue. *Volume 5: Mineral County, Nevada: Roads and Routes of the Past*. Museum Associates of Mineral County, 2012.

Silver, Sue. *Mineral County, Nevada: Volume 5, Roads and Routes of the Past*. Museum Associates of Mineral County, 2012.

Somerville, June Wood. *A Legend of a Road. A witness to the exploration and emigration on the road above Silver Lake and beyond*. June Wood Somerville, 2014.

Stewart, George R. *Ordeal by Hunger: The story of the Donner Party*. Houghton Mifflin Company, 1988.

Stewart, Robert E. *Aurora: Nevada's Ghost City of the Dawn*. Nevada Publications, 2004. Pages 67-70.

Stories from Mimi: The Water Works: Virginia City & Gold Hill, Nevada

Smith, Grant H. *The History of the Comstock Lode*. University of Nevada Press, 1997. Page 45.

The Natural Wealth of California: Comprising Early History; Geography, Topography, and Scenery; Climate; Agriculture and Commercial Products; Geology, Zoology, and Botany; Mineralogy, Mines, and Mining Processes; Manufactures; Steamship Lines, Railroads, and Commerce; Immigration, Population and Society; Educational Institutions and Literature; Together with a Detailed Description of Each County

Tortorich, Frank Jr. *Gold Rush Trail: A guide to the Carson River Route of the Emigrant Trail*. Wagon Wheel Tours, 1998.

Tortorich, Frank. John "Snowshoe" Thompson: Pioneer mail carrier of the Sierra. Pronghornpress, 2015.

Underwood, Brent. Ghost Town Living: Mining for purpose and chasing dreams at the edge of Death Valley. 2024.

Wakatskui Houston, Jeanne & James D. Houston. Farwell to Manzanar. Dell Laurel-Leaf. 1973.

Wedertz, Frank S. Mono Diggings. Historical Sketches of Old Bridgeport Big Meadows and Vicinity. Chalfant Press, 1978.

WEBSITES

Bureau of Land Management https://www.blm.gov

Clairitage Press https://www.clairitage.com

David Rumsey map Collection https://www.davidrumsey.com/luna/servlet/RUMSEY~8~1

Dennis Cassinelli: https://denniscassinelli.com

California Office of Historic Preservation https://ohp.parks.ca.gov

Donner Summit Historical Society https://www.donnersummithistoricalsociety.org/pages/petroglyphs.html

Exploring Lassen Counties Past https://www.citlink.net/~lahontan/susanville.htm

Great Basin Institute: Tallac Historic Site https://taylortallac.org/tallac-historic-site-home/

The Inn at Benton Hot Springs https://www.bentonhotsprings.us/

Lassen County Historical Society https://susanvillehistory.com

Legends of America: https://www.legendsofamerica.com

National Park Service https://www.nps.gov/index.htm

National Pony Express Association https://nationalponyexpress.org

Nevada Expeditions https://www.nvexpeditions.com/index.php

Nevada State Historical Society https://www.nvhistoricalsociety.org

Nevada State Library and Archives http://dmla.clan.lib.nv.us/docs/nsla/

Smithsonian Magazine https://www.smithsonianmag.com

University of Nevada Libraries https://library.unr.edu

Stewart Indian School https://stewartindianschool.com

US Forest Service: https://www.fs.usda.gov/recarea/ltbmu/recarea/?recid=11784
USGS https://www.usgs.gov

INDEX

AFTERWORD

I invite you to enjoy the rich heritage and beauty of the Eastern Sierra. Take only photographs and leave only footprints to preserve our historical resources. Please respect private property and our state and national lands. Various laws protect historical sites. Removing or damaging artifacts is illegal under federal and state laws. See the Archaeological Resources Protection Act (ARPA) for more information.

As always, be prepared when traveling. It has been over 175 years since the first emigrants traversed and settled this isolated land. Yet, the Eastern Sierra remains rugged and remote. Rocks and trees destroy vehicle tires as they did with pioneer wagon wheels. Water and food are always a concern, as with the Donner Party and the Lost '49ers. Early settlers' only communication with the outside world was by hand-carried paper. That remains true today; cell service is nonexistent in many locations.

Some sites are remote and require high clearance, 4-wheel drive vehicles, and hiking. Others are right off the highway. Whatever you drive, you can explore history along your journey.

Please follow me to see more ghost towns and historic sites in California and Nevada. You can find me at *Nevada Ghost Towns & Beyond* at NVTami.com, on Facebook at NVTami, on Instagram @NVTami, and on KGFN, Radio Goldfield, which you can stream on various websites.

I present at various historical and special interest groups. To request a presentation or participation at an event, email me at Tami@NVTami.com.

PHOTOS AND HISTORY BY TAMI FORCE

in the GLOW
of the SIERRA

GHOST TOWNS & HISTORICAL SITES OF THE
EASTERN SIERRA: SOUTHERN REGION

Continue your journey to the southern
region of the Eastern Sierra...

in the GLOW
of the SIERRA

THIS COMPANION BOOK COVERS GHOST TOWNS
AND HISTORICAL SITES FROM MONO COUNTY
THROUGH THE SOUTHERN TIP OF THE RANGE.